presented to
THE STUDENTS OF

Albright College

FOR USE IN

The Library

with the compliments of
THE PUBLISHERS

NEW YORK ABINGDON PRESS NASHVILLE

no middle ground

D0067885

"The Conference in the Crimea was a turning point in American history. There will soon be presented to the Senate and the American people a great decision which will determine the fate of the United States—and of the world—for generations to come. There can be no middle ground here."

Franklin Delano Roosevelt,
March 1, 1945, in an address
on the Crimean Conference
to the Congress of the
United States.

ROGER HUBER

no middle ground

A Celebration of the Liberation from Religion

✳

Introduction by George W. Webber

 ABINGDON PRESS
Nashville and New York

NO MIDDLE GROUND

Copyright © 1971 by Abingdon Press

All rights in this book are reserved.
No part of the book may be reproduced in any
manner whatsoever without written permission of
the publishers except brief quotations embodied in
critical articles or reviews. For information address
Abingdon Press, Nashville, Tennessee.

ISBN 0-687-28033-8

Library of Congress Catalog Card Number: 78-158675

Scripture quotations unless otherwise noted are from the Revised Standard
Version of the Bible, copyrighted 1946 and 1952 by the Division of
Christian Education, National Council of Churches, and are used by per-
mission.

Quotations from *The Greening of America* by Charles A. Reich, copy-
right © October 1970 by Random House, Inc., originally published as
"Reflections—The Greening of America" in *The New Yorker Magazine,*
Sept. 26, 1970, are used by permission of Random House, Inc. and
The New Yorker.

Quotations from *The Secular City* by Harvey Cox, copyright © Harvey
Cox 1965 are used by permission of the Publishers, The Macmillan
Company, New York, and Collier-Macmillan Canada Ltd., Toronto.

Quotations from *Letters and Papers from Prison* by Dietrich Bonhoeffer,
copyright © The Macmillan Company 1953, rev. ed. 1967, and © SCM
Press Ltd. 1967, are reprinted by permission of The Macmillan Company
and SCM Press Ltd.

Excerpts from "Let's Be Honest About the Canon" by Richard Lyon
Morgan, copyright © 1967 Christian Century Foundation, are reprinted by
permission from the May 31, 1967 issue of *The Christian Century.*

Excerpts from "Human First, Christian Second" by Michael Novak, copyright © 1968 Christian Century Foundation, are reprinted by permission
from the June 19, 1968 issue of *The Christian Century.*

Excerpts from "The Meaning of Membership" by Robert C. Dodds, copyright © 1968 Christian Century Foundation, are reprinted by permission
from the September 11, 1968 issue of *The Christian Century.*

SET UP, PRINTED, AND BOUND BY
THE PARTHENON PRESS, AT NASHVILLE,
TENNESSEE, UNITED STATES OF AMERICA

263
H 877m

132066

for Bess
who saves me daily from being religious
and in so doing creates the possibility of
being Christian

contents

introduction

I am tired of books on renewal. But out of concern for a fellow clergyman I agreed to read the manuscript of *No Middle Ground*. The process was unmistakably enthralling and genuinely rewarding. For Roger Huber has written not only from the heart but with insight and power about the issues that are today crippling the churches and creating the "gathering storm." This book will neither comfort clergy nor turn off laymen: it should profoundly provoke and challenge both.

In my present work in theological education, I encounter two recurring problems expressed by those who are the church. Clergy complain bitterly or miserably about the unwillingness of their people to accept the implications of commitment to Jesus Christ. Each month now, through the office of *Bearings for Reestablishment* in our seminary building, some one hundred nuns and clergy, many Protestants among them, seek help in moving to new vocations. Such is their level of frustration. At the same time, I keep encountering among the laity a terrible dis-ease over the fact that they joined the church under one clear set of ground rules, and now the game the clergy wish them to play has changed so drastically they are tempted to drop out and forget the whole thing. Roger Huber is writing about this very central question for Christians in our time: If we say that Jesus Christ is Lord, if we center our self-understanding on that confession and in that Person, what are the consequences? Huber's point is simply that we are called into a total way of life that has implications not only for a man's present commitments, but also opens up before him new responsibilities and creates new relationships.

The primary question, then, is the meaning of personal commitment and obedience. Is one called to accept a Lord who promises salvation, security, wholeness, a new family that provides community in an impersonal or hostile world? Or does obedience to Jesus Christ call a man to a new vocation, not to a salvation status, but to be a soldier in the missionary work of his Lord? This rather simple alternative does not do justice to the thoughtful and sensitive way in which Huber confronts us with this question and explores it in such a way that we cannot avoid its thrust and bite. He calls the difference he is getting at the distinction between religion and Christianity. Religion exists to explain life's meaning, to provide a man with a center of security. All men have religion, consciously or unconsciously. It is the basis on which they make their decisions, determine their priorities, the object of their loyalty and devotion, whatever the form it takes. But Christianity stands over against all religions. Although it provides meaning and perspective, it is a calling to turn one's life inside out, to find one's life in losing it, to join a pilgrim people whose task is the care of God's world, with the freedom that comes only when self-preoccupation is undercut by a new loyalty.

The secondary question is one of ecclesiology. In religion, the church exists to take care of its members. The clergyman is the mother, called to tend and comfort her flock. They gather for the ritual acts that keep alive their common life, their memories and hopes. In the church are centered religious activities and meaning. There is a sacred place, God's house where he is worshiped. But in Christianity the church is the base out of which Christians operate. It has a different style and quality. Now it is a place of nurture, where the recruit in the band of God's pilgrim people gets his boot camp training, discovers the discipline that mission requires, and gains the habits that will be needed in meeting his responsibilities. The clergy serve as those who equip the people of God for what happens on the road. The church finds its center outside its own life. The clergy are only functionaries, servants to the servants of Christ.

The poignancy of the present moment in the life of the

churches arises from the terrible desire to find a way of holding both positions together, to find a happy compromise or middle ground. This is the source of great anguish. And I fear it cannot be done. Religion and Christianity are antithetical. The church is either concentric or ex-centric. The attempt to hold both even in creative tension is only to compound frustration and lead to total incapacity to serve any of the needs of men, whether as religion or as Christianity.

I find myself embarrassed at the inadequacies of what I have written to get at the winsome and yet compelling force of Huber's analysis of our profound commitment to religion, when we thought we were all the time committed to Jesus and his church.

GEORGE W. WEBBER
President, New York Theological Seminary
New York City

preface

We were at the seashore on holiday six years ago when we learned that my wife had and has an incurable, potentially crippling disease called multiple sclerosis. There is a decisive connection between that and the fact that this book is about the creation of a revolution in the church for, of, and by laymen; indeed, between that and the fact that the book was written at all.

The frailty produced in her body was such that I was needed a lot at home. With the help and encouragement of our many friends in the Riverdale Presbyterian Church in New York City, of which I was then the minister, I rearranged my schedule and activities, one result being that I did almost no preaching for a three-month period. During that time this book, whose purpose is to create a revolution in the church, began to take shape in my mind. Although I had many worries centering around the baffling discouragement of my wife's illness, I also had time to think about other matters. One object of reflection was the past—the communities I had known, the churches I had served, the people with whom I had lived and worked.

In fresh ways I saw that past as a richly varied mosaic of human experience. Just out of seminary there were three years as an assistant in a central city church in an eastern metropolis; two years of study in Scotland; another five in a Pennsylvania industrial town on the Delaware River; another six in an affluent Westchester County suburb, and finally, in 1963, a church in the Riverdale section of New York City. Those places represented the major landmarks of my adult life. As I thought of them in great detail, I was then and am now, six years later, immensely grateful that those landmarks were so different. Each one possessed of singular shape and contour.

Yet, diversely rich as my experience had been, I was deeply

disturbed by a common bond of feeling that somehow held all those years together and made them one. I don't know how best to describe that feeling. Part of it was regret. Part of it was intense awareness that something precious had been wasted. Was it the years? Was it my talent? Was it my interest? Was it my ministry? Was it my very life?

As I reflected on what I was going through I gradually moved toward clarity and insight by isolating the factors which were *not* the primal cause of my personal crisis. Although gravely worried and sometimes depressed by the fact of serious illness in the family, I knew it was not that. Nor was it personal in the sense of being a marriage-oriented or child-oriented wound that hurt me so. For I happen, by some marvelous turn of providence or luck, to be married to a woman through whose life I have come to grasp most of what I know about love and courage. We have five children who are healthy, reasonably well behaved, creatively alienated from the prevailing culture, and whose spirits are still free. Like every other family that ever was, we have learned some immensely valuable things the hard way. But that is integral to the blessing. Clearly, I had to look elsewhere for the source of the overwhelming feeling that something precious had been wasted, and the related feeling of massive regret.

My being forced to live with emotional reality was not because my work in the ministry, judged by generally accepted standards, had been a failure. Quite the contrary. As such things are usually measured, my years in the ministry had been "successful" ones. Like hundreds and thousands of Protestant ministers, I had in recent years been through the whole institutional bit—growing membership rolls, expanding budgets, evolving and expanding programs, major property renovations, new church school building erected, new manse paid for, old mortgages burned, new sets of officers trained, new techniques tried, etc. Along the way I had made my share of lifelong friends, and had never experienced the agony of tormented personal or congregational dissension in getting it all done.

Some lives were influenced in ways that mattered, deeply. I received more than my deserved share of praise for certain aspects of my work; there was authentic gratitude for many of the things I had tried to do and be.

But with all those reasons to be grateful and confident, I still had that irrepressible awareness of massive regret about those seemingly productive years—regret that something precious had been wasted. Gradually, and with the felt ambivalence of wanted yet not wanted discovery, I knew that what had been wasted was the years themselves—some of the best years of my life. Gone. Irretrievably. Slowly and painfully, yet also with a sense of dawning joy, I was able to define and delimit the precise sense in which those years were wasted. They were wasted exactly because the truths articulated in this book had not been the foundations of my ministry. Those truths had not determined its style; they had not established its priorities. The absence of those informing truths bound together my experience in central Philadelphia, in rural Scotland, in industrial Chester, in suburban Scarborough, and in metropolitan New York. Their absence had created the feeling of immense wastage and over-whelming regret.

"Absence" is perhaps too strong a word. For I had talked about and preached about these insights off and on all through the years. I had not been a total stranger to them. Nor had my ministry been totally devoid of their influence. But my ministry and my whole life had been substantially uninfluenced by them. The result was irrepressible awareness of unproductive waste and poignant regret.

I have set this book in a personal context because such data should make it clear that the exceedingly judgmental things I write about the church and the ministry are directed, first of all, at myself and my own ministry. I could easily write a second book supplying the evidence, if any were needed.

But there is another acutely important reason for focusing attention on these personal data. I am now deeply convinced that there are hundreds, probably thousands, of clergymen and

15

thousands, probably tens of thousands, of laymen who have essentially the same feelings and for essentially the same reasons. They may not label those feelings as I have labeled them—"wastage" and "regret." They may not affirm the absence of God's life from their lives with the same words. Indeed, I suspect that more often those feelings are experienced by members of the emerging revolutionary community as longing, yearning, and a profound sense of unfulfillment about their lives in the church. But however they are labeled, however experienced, however articulated, the reality from which those crucial feelings spring is there, welling up irrespressibly in countless minds and hearts. The emergence of those feelings is an identifying characteristic of our time. I believe those feelings are the human ingredients with which God himself will resurrect the church from its present death. Could it be that those feelings are creations of God himself?

I believe they are. I would like to bet my life that they are.

One result of such belief and desire is the following conviction: A great need of the moment is for all men and women who have these accrued feelings of unfulfillment about their lives in the church to find one another, to strengthen one another, to support and help one another. For what we can never do alone as solo performers, we can do together in the Body of Christ. All such men and women need one another. I make bold to hope that this book will help bring us together and enable us to accelerate the processes of responsible revolution in the church.

At this moment in history, bringing off a revolution in the institutional church feels like an unbearably lonely business. A frightening one, too. None of us can predict what it will mean in our personal lives, or in the lives of our loved ones. In the presence of that sometimes terrifying uncertainty, the felt loneliness-in-fear often saps our courage and with overwhelming power tempts us to turn back and go on minding the store.

We must not let that turning back occur. We cannot. The

revolution in the church is already happening. No longer is there any question of its reality. For individuals, the only remaining question is one about the nature, extent, and quality of our involvement. It is characteristic of revolutions that they make nonparticipation impossible. In a revolution there are no spectators, only participants.

Therefore as we participate in this "happening of God" we must remember several things. None of us deserves to be part of this rebirth. We all are frail and fallible, and the record is not good. But in spite of that, the compelling fact remains: We do have the chance to participate. We are free. We can opt for resurrection.

Another matter relates to opposition. When some people resist the changes we believe God is calling the church to make, when they demean our motives or threaten our security, we must remember that their opposition is often rooted in the reality of our own lives. It is a gross oversimplification to say or think that they are always being perversely obstructionist or too enslaved by the past. Often they look at our lives, our actual performance, and then, on the basis of what they see, quite properly call in question our right to disturb the peace. We revolutionaries must make it clear in what we say and do that we disturb the peace not because we have seen a vision and obeyed it, but precisely because we have seen a vision and *long* to obey it, with them, in their much-needed, deeply desired company.

As the revolution develops we need also to bear in mind the separateness of institutions from the individuals who are their constituents. Of course it is true that institutions are made up of individuals. But it is equally true that institutions somehow have an identity of their own. Therefore we must repeatedly make it clear that severe judgments on institutions are not necessarily total, or even significantly partial, judgments on the personal lives of the individuals whose work or interest is largely related to those institutions. One of the abiding mysteries is that as individuals in our personal lives we frequently operate by standards considerably higher than those to which we give consent in institutional settings. Institutionally we often approve all manner of procedure, practice, and priority we would not approve in our private lives. This is a crucial distinction, for it helps us remember that attacks on institutions should not be made and understood as attacks on individual persons. So to make them or interpret them is at once naïve, dishonest, irresponsible, and counterrevolutionary.

Additionally we must consider this: The process of discovering one another, of pooling the felt unfulfillment of our lives in the church, will surely create many new friendships. Initially some persons will be less responsive to revolutionary impulse, not because they feel the longing for renewal less deeply than others, but because their energies are drained away carrying the burdens of responsibility for the institution as we now have it. Those who create revolutionary change are not intrinsically better men and women, but they are often freer precisely because they have been less responsible institutionally. Erich Fromm is clearly right when he observes that persons fully committed to existing institutions are relatively less free to anticipate the kind and quality of change those institutions must undergo, and to bring it about.

This essential insight will save responsible revolutionaries from self-righteous, arrogant criticism of opponents who may well be their moral superiors. It will also help those who have carried heavy institutional responsibility over the years to welcome the appearance of disturbing ideas, troubling disruptive possibilities, and to recognize those who advocate them as brothers, not competitors or critics or judges or enemies.

However, not only in the church can revolutionaries look for allies. It is also, indeed more so, in the world that kindred spirits will be found. For it is one of the many blessings of a truly secular society that God's faithful servants shall pervade it. They shall be found in every phase and facet of its incredibly challenging complexity. We can hold ourselves open to an exciting probability: Some of the most sensitively spiritual and prophetically Christian leadership will come to us in the approaching decades from secularly oriented businessmen, labor leaders, physicians, artists, politicians, educators, attorneys, and scientists. Nearly all such leaders will be what we now call "laymen." In the Church Alive we shall recognize their leadership. We shall learn to sit at their feet while they tell us, often unknowingly, of the things which pertain to God. The gathering together of that revolutionary, lay-leadership community constitutes the only hope the church now has for survival. That hope is what this book is about.

It is a book which affirms that change is a law of life—not change advocated or implemented as an end in itself, but rather that special brand of change for which the gospel of Christ provides both a personal and an institutional dynamic. Relying on that dynamic, this book is offered as a field manual for that growing company of men and women whose faith commits them to the revolutionary proposition that the church's determination to change, and change radically, is the primary index of its well-being.

Many people helped me with the preparation of this manuscript. I want to name but two for whom I am especially grateful. One is Doris Foster; her steady competence and hopeful encouragement were unfailing throughout the typing of three of four versions. The other is Norman Dewire, Executive Director of The Joint Strategy and Action Committee; as we talked the book through together his thought constantly challenged my own. His commitment to its central ideas is an auspicious sign of the times.

Montclair, New Jersey
December 1970

1   John and Bill

If a vision is a moment when one really sees for the first time something he has looked at a thousand times before, then I had a vision in October 1969, in the act of answering the phone. At the other end of the line was John (names, circumstances, and details are changed for obvious reasons).

Pleasantries were exchanged before the nominating committee was mentioned almost casually. Most Protestant churches have these annually functioning nominating committees. Their job is to select the lay leadership of the church by submitting a list of persons chosen to run the institutional show. Once nominated, it is virtually certain they will be elected.

In response to John's question about how the work of the nominating committee was going, I replied, "Well, I've attended only one of their meetings, so I don't know the details, but as you know, it's a great group of people and they're taking their job seriously." By "great" I meant, in part, "representative," for the committee included many shades of feeling and opinion on the liberal-conservative spectrum. By "great" I also meant "strongly effective," for each member of that key group, from the most conservative to the most liberal, was like every other in the sense of having large measures of intelligence and integrity.

John's tone became more serious. "What I'm really wondering about is Bill."

"What about Bill?" I asked, knowing the answer.

"C'mon Roger, you know what I mean. A lot of us who've been around Central Church a long time are going to be very upset if Bill's nominated as an Elder."

The grapevine and human nature being what they are, John knew before he called me that I had attended that one meeting of the nominating committee for an openly political reason:

to explain as best I could what I thought was happening in the church, in the world, and why in consequence I felt certain persons should be given careful consideration by them in the completion of their committee's task. After sharing thoughts and feelings about those matters and about the meaning of leadership in such a context, I submitted a list of names with the request that they think seriously about each person on the list. At the top of that list was Bill, because Bill incorporates in his life, thought, and understanding ideas on whose implementation the survival of the church in our time depends. (Bill was discussed and not nominated in the course of the committee's work.)

"Why are you going to be upset, John?"

"Well, Roger, it's not so much that I'm gonna be upset. Bill's fine and I don't have a thing against him. I understand his activism, and I like him. In a few years I'm sure he'll be one of Central's best leaders, but right now a lot of us think he just isn't ready for the Session of Central Church. I don't have to tell you that many people think he's too radical."

Our conversation ground to a slow, steady halt, with felt measures of fatigue on both sides. John and I had tried on many previous occasions, not too successfully, to shape each other's minds on matters germane to the future of the church. He was not very good at sounding casual with a closing suggestion that I not twist the committee's arm about Bill. I replied, "Well, John, you know where I stand on that one. If we care about the church at all, we'd better start thanking God for guys like Bill."

Thus ended one more episode in a power struggle that is now tearing the church apart. This power struggle is happening throughout American Protestantism and threatens to destroy the whole church. Most of the episodes in that struggle are as undramatic as the one just described, but underneath all the gentlemanly politeness there is a shared awareness that everything about the past and future of the church is now at stake. John and Bill both know that the issue separating them

22

is nothing less than the survival of the church. Around that issue each in his own way is playing for keeps.

Lest that judgment be misinterpreted, it is essential to describe both John and Bill. Bill first, then John.

Bill is thirty years old. He is an honors graduate of a prestigious university. He has an uncommonly intelligent wife, two children, a forty-thousand-dollar home not paid for, and a promising future on the management team of a major, rapidly growing industry. His appearance would not cause a stir in the dining room of Philadelphia's Union League. In ten years he will probably be a senior vice president of his company. He is on his way up and, for him, there is undoubtedly room at the top. He still wants that place, but it now seems much less important to him and less desirable than it did when he first joined the company. In his genuine leather attaché case he carries not only management studies and staff reports, but also books like *The Greening of America*, and *The Feast of Fools*, and *The Making of a Counterculture*. Moreover, he devours such books on the commuter bus which carries him every morning into Manhattan and back again at night to Montclair. Such books upset him and often anger him, but he keeps on reading them, because Bill has come to a point where he has to make more sense of, and find more meaning in, his own life. Such reading sometimes seems to help him do that.

John is fifty-nine years old. He is an honors graduate of a prestigious university. He has an uncommonly intelligent wife, three children, and a seventy-thousand-dollar house paid for. For ten years he has been executive vice president of the company he joined on graduating from college. In the business world, in the community, in the church, he has been significantly involved in a long list of responsible, forward-looking programs, activities, and developments. He is one of the most respected men in the community, and I, too, have high personal regard for him. John honestly, genuinely, believes it would be destructive for Bill to be elected to the Central Church Session, even though the outward circumstances of

23

132066

their lives bear many similarities and their life styles close resemblance.

Why?

Because John and Bill, even though their paths cross frequently, live in two different worlds. Those worlds are built with two disparate sets of experience, two sometimes diametrically opposed systems of value, two variant readings of history, two conflicting sets of priorities, two hugely contradictory understandings of the Bible, the meaning of faith, and the qualities of mind and heart which make for responsible leadership in the church. Commitment to the church is important in both their lives and taken seriously. But they are not friends. They do not believe in each other. They do not trust, understand, or love each other. They are alienated. In the current lingo, they are polarized.

John and Bill are at odds in the world and in the church because John, at fifty-nine, is underprivileged; his whole life experience has not equipped him to understand what Bill, at thirty, grasps with increasing clarity about the meaning of history and the content of the gospel. To make this necessary distinction is not a moral judgment, for Bill is not "finer," or more intelligent or in any moral way better than John, but he is more alive, more aware, more nearly free and, in the mystery of life, luckier. John came to his adult years in a time when the church, through teaching and training him to be "religious," diminished significantly by the time of his advanced middle age whatever capacity and skill he may earlier have had for discerning what Jesus once identified as "the signs of the times."

John is the finished and nearly perfect product of a corrupt system.

Bill is the unfinished product of that system's collapse.

To say that they hate each other is language too strong; to suggest that they misunderstand each other is a euphemism for something midway between alienation and hatred; to say that they experience each other in the context of threat is objective description; to insist that they need each other is a masterpiece of understatement; to affirm that they can find each other, support each other, and together bring the church of Christ into creative rapport with what is happening in history is to believe that they can both come of age. So to believe is to purvey hope in the crucible of a nearly hopeless situation.

John thinks he is about to transfer his membership elsewhere because Central Church is not spiritual enough, not religious enough, too activist and political and involved. But he can't quite do it because there is no place to go—institutionally his choices are limited to a few churches even worse than Central when judged by the inadequacies just listed, or to the great majority of churches which his deep, instinctual integrity tells him are already dead. Moreover, John loves Central Church; a lot of his life and love are invested there.

Bill is also about to leave Central Church. He feels that John and his friends are affable enough but quietly determined not to share their power—the power to make decisions and establish priorities. Although young, Bill also feels he has a limited supply of strength and that it is bad stewardship to spend it on institutions which will not gladly embrace the discipline of substantive change. His best efforts to help Central Church change have been rebuffed, ignored, sneered at, or held in utter contempt, and he is profoundly discouraged. That discouragement has pressed him to the very edges of the church's life, and soon we will have lost him entirely.

The pathos of this situation is that Christ is important to both these men. In response to what they believe to be the demands on their lives made by a common Lord and Savior, both are moving away from Central Church. John is doing it by staying home, reducing his pledge, feeling hurt, misunderstood, unappreciated, angry. Bill is doing it by giving more and more of his time, talent, and treasure to secular movements and causes which seem to implement his understanding of a nonreligious gospel. In those activities he feels the authentic joy which properly belongs to a fellowship of those who

25

love in the service of those who suffer. Both are unhappy men, for their alienation has not wholly eroded their felt need for each other. Both are deeply frustrated, for neither can quite admit to the other that both are living in a no-man's-land, between two worlds, one dead, the other powerless to be born.

Multiply John and Bill by an unknown factor of millions, and you have a viable image of the gathering storm in the churches—a storm that may indeed destroy the church.

And the clergy. Where are we in the midst of this tragic polarization?

Someplace in that same storm looking for safe harbor, someplace in that same no-man's-land trying to transform it into a protected middle ground, hoping to survive until the storm ends and the battle is over, that is, until retirement makes it possible for us to be noncombatants, veterans drawing our pensions.

But for us clergy, that kind of middle ground is not a living place. It is literally, fundamentally, theologically, existentially a dead center, a wellspring of everything that negates life, especially life in Christ.

If there is hope for the church in our time, it inheres importantly in an intricacy of acts and commitments through which we who are its professionals shall abandon that safe middle and take sides with Bill by empowering him, establishing him, and training him as a revolutionary in the church. This does not mean putting the life of the church in a win-lose context, like an old Western movie where the good guys just have to prevail over the baddies. Especially this does not mean wiping John out, for Bill is not better than John in any moralistic sense. Indeed, in many ways John has a much better performance record than Bill, and I want to be counted as one who perceives clearly and appreciates deeply the many qualities of towering strength present and operative in John's life. Taking sides with Bill does not mean being insensitive to John's many strengths. It just means that the act of commitment is central to an experience of gospel power, and the clergy cannot

26

forever pretend their primary function in the polarization of the church to be that of mediators or reconcilers. Taking sides with Bill cannot be done personally. It must be done on the level of the issues. In the present extreme crisis to speak of reconciling the polarized camps in the church is usually to cop out, to quit, to become at best paralyzed, and at worst disobedient or heretical or apostate or all three. If reconciliation is the ministry we are called to, surely it is a ministry we enter through the narrow, disciplined gate of commitment. The nature of that discipline and the substance of that commitment, for clergy and laymen alike, are spelled out in the later chapters of this field manual for revolutionaries. At this point, let it suffice to affirm that their essential content is risk. For discipline and the commitment equally demand that all Christians shall not withdraw from the struggle. We must all take sides on the issues, as those issues are inescapably before us, come hell or high water.

It will probably be both. And in the searing context of that both-ness the religious professional will survive only in the measure that he is mature enough and personally, inwardly secure enough to keep the issues depersonalized. When he takes the tensions personally as intended threat, he becomes an enemy of God's revolution and succeeds disastrously in revealing his own paranoia. When powerful members of his congregation threaten to undo him, he must be big enough to grasp, dynamically, that they are not threatened by him, nor are they reacting to him. Rather, they are threatened by, even as he is threatened by, and reacting to, even as he is reacting to, the felt collapse of an entire value system; they are reacting to the historical death of a whole understanding of life as an event in their lives, and the failure of a consequent life style—a life style belonging to clergy and cherished by clergy no less than by laymen. That collapse, that death, that failure, and the possibility of a completely new perception are what the gospel, experienced, has always been about. In Christ the old is passed away. Behold, there is a new creation.

27

Rebirth in Christ is simultaneously joyous and scary. For clergy and laymen alike it is the source of glorious days and sleepless nights. In part it is scary because one has not only the joy of being new in Christ but also the reality of paying bills and educating children and trying to provide for the future. It is not easy to retool, not easy to make a series of lateral or descending moves economically, not easy to teach an old dog new tricks, not simple even to consider fulfilling one's ordination vows by learning to support a family in a secular vocation. No true servant of the revolution is a stranger to fear.

I felt that fear with force in the spring of 1970. Naïvely I had been going along on the assumption that the polarization in Central Church was a healthy one being conducted on the basis of the issues as delineated in this field manual. It was one of the greatest shocks of my life to be told by a friend in the church that all through the spring meetings had been held in living rooms around the community. Ostensibly the agenda for these meetings was the question: How can we unify Central Church? But, my friend assured me, the unspoken agenda was the consideration of quite a different question: How can the *source* of the disunity be dealt with, or toned down, or removed? Clearly many persons had come to perceive me as that source, rather than the issues.

One man for whom I have deep respect and admiration wrote to me in June 1970 and said among other things about his own and his wife's feelings: "We are aware of the many meetings of our fellow members (we have attended only one) which have been held, and we believe these members feel strongly that you do not realize their frustration about urging you to take steps to reunite and strengthen our church."

In such a setting I did indeed feel disappointed and angry and frightened and, in my worst moments, attacked. But letting those feelings dominate one's thought and action is kid stuff for little boys, not for men, especially not for men come of age. So I tried not to personalize the conflict. By and large that effort has been successful. When I have had a

28

decent night's sleep, I know my antagonists in the church do not dislike me as a person, but they are profoundly traumatized by what I stand for. On a purely personal basis it is increasingly clear that many of the most upset people like me genuinely, and that their upsetness is intensified by their inability to understand how a person they perceive as such a nice guy could betray them by calling their whole value-system life-style status-quo preserving syndrome in question in the name of Christ.

Their anxiety is also heightened by their certain knowledge, in the deep places, of my elemental respect and honest love for them. So far my position has remained tenable because they know, with a species of inalienable certainty, that I in my mind and heart do not wipe them out as persons. With an authentic perception not to be destroyed by all their lifelong exposures to phony religion, they know I am aware of and reasonably honest about my own frailties, that I am sensitive to and appreciative of their strengths, that my affection for them is the real article. Moreover, and crucially, they are beginning to read, because it is now written so plainly across the whole of human experience, the handwriting on history's wall. My antagonists know that our conflict is not personal, that it centers around seminally inescapable questions: What is happening? What does the turbulence of our time signify? Is God in it and of it, or is he not? What does Scripture say it is all about? In the context of struggle raised by these agonizing inquiries, I have survived because my antagonists in the church now know that on these matters I will not tell them lies, not even when the lies are those which for generation piled on generation have been sanctified by the church. I realize that they, too, are in profound agony. After all, it is traumatic, ultimately traumatic to realize, or even to begin realizing that your spiritual mother is a whore.

Inside Bill that recognition is conscious, painful, and he is dealing with it. His inner transactions with that recognition are tempting him to withdraw from the conflict. That possibility, withdrawal, is tragic because Bill's intelligence, sophistication, and commitment are the ingredients of a desperately needed revolution in the church.

Inside John that recognition is not conscious. Consequently it is not being dealt with. Indeed, John's awareness of Bill's recognition of the church's whoredom is the very thing that alienates John from Bill. This is also tragic, for John's intelligence, sophistication, and commitment are also desperately needed for the revolution. Both John and Bill have immense, nearly unlimited resources to invest in that happening of God. At this moment in history it is not likely that the church will receive what Bill has to give because Bill is so demoralized by the church's love affair with its own sickness. But receiving similar gifts of self from John is even less likely, for John honestly believes that sickness to be health. John calls sickness health for many reasons, not the least of which is the controlling influence in his life of an immensely powerful myth. That myth has given him a "religious," spiritual rationale for the church's diseased condition, enabled him to say yes to it, to increase its virulence. John is, indeed, captive to that myth. Therefore, to love John, to believe him a child of God, to long for his deep involvement in the Church Alive requires of us that we examine, in some detail, his imprisoning myth.

II   The Imprisoning Myth

In the early 1930s when America endured the agony of the Great Depression, I was a boy. I did not understand exactly what was going on, but I felt what was happening, as did millions of young people. My father was the owner of a small business in an Iowa farming town, an enterprise he had built with much hard work. When the Great Depression hit the nation my father lost everything he had saved. In the midst of that crisis, I remember the feel of many conversations among older members of the family about whether, when, and under what circumstances my father's store would be closed. The depression-oriented problems of other people in town were also discussed.

Listening in, one thing I picked up was that many hard-working men in town had lost their savings, their jobs, and that there was no work to do, at least in the sense of paying jobs. These were men I knew. I had been in their homes, I had greeted them daily in the streets and on Sunday in church, I went to school with their children and played in their back yards. It was about these men that I gradually developed insight. Feeling rather than careful articulation is characteristic for a boy's mind, so I never spelled it out rationally. But the insight was there, in me. What I gradually absorbed during those hard, lean years was that men in large numbers can be underemployed or unemployed through no fault of their own. In my own boyish way I began to understand that basically fine, good men could become discouraged, indolent, demoralized, even self-destructive, and not be responsible for it. I saw that men can and do become the victims of circumstances beyond their control, and that it is an act of cruelty to say to such men, trapped in such circumstances: "Straighten up and fly right." During the Depression millions of Americans could not do that without massive outside help, even though they were ambitious, frugal, responsible, hard-working men. That is what I learned early and never forgot.

Unfortunately it is that same truth which as a society we have not learned and never really believed. As a society we are still operating inside the limitations of something called "the Protestant ethic." And what is that ethic? It is a large part of our conscious and unconscious mental furniture. It is an intricately interwoven web of largely unquestioned assumptions about the nature of man and the qualities of the good life, assumptions rooted in an emphasis on individual effort as the be-all and end-all of our human existence, assumptions which assign ultimate worth to such qualities of character as initiative, cleverness, thrift, and personal enterprise.

The Protestant ethic enshrines intense individualism. There are competent scholars like Max Weber, the German social theorist of fifty years ago, who suggest that it was this Protestant ethic of intense individualism which more than any other motivating force in the nineteenth century gave rise to modern, industrial, laissez-faire capitalism. Historically what happened was that the Protestant ethic and the industrial revolution got married. In many ways that marriage was good, especially in America. That partnership taught men to lift themselves by their own bootstraps and became one of the foundation stones on which our fathers and grandfathers built the wealthiest nation in all human history. Wealth is not intrinsic curse. It is potential blessing, and the qualities of human character it produces are not to be wholly condemned. But life is never lacking in ambiguity, and all blessings are, therefore, mixed.

The Protestant ethic is a classic case in point. In many ways that ethic has become more "a defense of the strong against the weak than an expression of Christian compassion, more a glorification of the individual than an illumination of Christian responsibility. . . , more a commercial ideology than a Christian doctrine of man. . . ." That harsh indictment comes not from any secular source but from the Presbyterian General

Assembly's Special Committee on the Church, the Christian, and Work. The counts in the indictment pile up as the report continues: The Protestant ethic "correctly discerns the indivduality of man, but does not grasp the depth of his involvement in the human community. An ethic for work cannot remain content with describing the virtue of an individual in the marketplace, because the character of the marketplace affects what a man can be and do. This is the fundamental weakness of our popularized 'Protestant Ethic': it refuses to move to a serious consideration of social order." Life-giving as it has been in many ways, the traditional Protestant work ethic has also had something profoundly death-dealing about it because it has ignored, and has taught laymen like John to ignore, the interdependent dimensions of our lives, dimensions just as decisive as the individual ones.

The Protestant work ethic has, therefore, become a mixed blessing whose limitations we must now recognize and overcome and help John to overcome, because it does not enable us, encourage us, or even permit us to grasp, respond to, and deal intelligently with the fact that my father, along with millions of men like him in the 1930s, were "down and out," even though they were classic examples of all those virtues the Protestant work ethic exalts: thrift, industry, ambition, initiative, and personal enterprise. By encouraging us to understand ourselves and one another as individuals rather than as members of the human community, the Protestant ethic has failed us, deceived us, given us splendid rationale for selfish irresponsibility. How? By blinding us to the fact that basically fine, good men can become discouraged, indolent, demoralized, and destructive through no fault of their own. The Protestant ethic has blinded John to the fact that circumstances can and do become so massive in their dehumanizing power, so crippling and overwhelming, that all moralizing exhortations to embrace the individualistic virtues of the Protestant ethic become a cruel, inhuman joke.

John does not understand—his church has not taught him

33

to understand—that the social, corporate, community dimension of our human life is a foundation stone of Christian faithfulness. He reads his morning paper and senses that the whole social structure is indeed crumbling, but he does not understand the relationship between that collapse and the myth which imprisons him. He is not free to be God's servant in a secular world because the popularized Protestant ethic undergirding his life and informing his religion never helped him understand that social order and social justice are the prime conditions of community and, in consequence, irreducible dimensions of faith in Jesus Christ. John is angered by and denies the very essence of that report to the Presbyterian General Assembly: "Our present increasingly complex economy is a corporate enterprise. It is based on the drawing together of materials, machines, power, processes and men for production, marketing and services. Any economic-social arrangement which gives access to those elements of economic activity and affords opportunity for occupational life to some, and denies access and opportunity to others violates community and is contrary to Christian faithfulness." By failing to create that insight, and by failing to help John implement the insight as prime evidence of his faith in Christ, the church has enshrined the Protestant ethic and given it the power of a dangerous and destructive myth; indeed, the church has made it the favorite myth of middle-American Protestant laymen.

There is a particular reason for being concerned about the destructive potential of the Protestant ethic in American life today. It relates to the alleged "war on poverty." The brittle fact is that there is no war on poverty; at best there is a polite skirmish with poverty. Why? Because Middle America's energy source, its controlling myth, is that ethic. It taught John that poverty is finally to be understood not as social failure, but as personal failure. John's religion says that poverty—and the whole intricate web of its consequences for man's common life—is tangible evidence of individual weakness, individual laziness, individual irresponsibility. Deep in the subconscious

34

levels of the American experience is a conviction that it is somehow an evidence of moral strength to succeed economically, and of moral weakness to fail economically. Result: it is widely considered not quite "moral," not really "American," somehow a compromise of the American way, an abandonment of the national religion, to declare war on poverty and to wage that war relentlessly with all the resources the nation possesses. To undo that complex of value judgments with all its concomitant priorities would be the work of a whole nation, but it will have to be energized by Middle American Protestant laymen. It will be incredibly difficult, perhaps as difficult as crawling back inside our mothers' wombs and trying to be born again, for the tens of millions of John's coreligionists in middle and upper middle-class America to demand that our nation wage massive war on poverty and on all its dehumanizing consequences. For what they really, subconsciously lean on all the time is an inner assurance that waging such a war would be the same thing as teaching people to be lazy and shiftless and irresponsible by giving them something they did not earn. Even though a failure to wage all-out war on poverty may destroy the nation, it will be hugely difficult to conduct such a war, precisely because the imprisoning myth is not narrowly religious or economic in scope. That myth was fatally injected into the bloodstream of America by the churches, but it is no longer confined to the churches. It now permeates the whole body of American life. The Protestant ethic is a genuinely national myth.

The shifting of gears from "Protestant ethic" to "national myth" is a matter of accuracy. For while it is true that this intensely community-denying individualism did have its origins in certain distortions of Calvinism, it has long since ceased to be a primarily theological phenomenon and has become a broadly cultural, uniquely national one. In many ways that is what made America great. The self-tightened belt and the self-supporting bootstrap are proudly worn by countless mil-

35

lions of middle-class Americans who, like John, have "made it." That belt and those bootstraps are the holy, sacred symbols of our national religion—a religion devoutly embraced not only by Protestants, but also by Jews, Catholics, agnostics, atheists. That religion is, empirically, what binds middle and upper middle-class America together; that binding power is what creates the only existentially ecumenical faith there is in America today.

As the Protestant ethic lost its roots in the Reformation, as it culturally evolved into a national religion of intense, self-reliant individuals, it blinded us to the following probability: If the millions of our fellow-citizens trapped in the urban and rural ghettos of America were enterprising, self-reliant, hard-working, thrifty and all the other things our national religion tells us men ought to be, and if they practiced those virtues intensively for a hundred years, the ghettos with all their obscene dehumanizations would still be there and would, indeed, have grown. Why? Because poverty is merely the best evidence there is that no man is an island entire of itself. Poverty is final evidence that all men belong to one another, that God really has turned the vineyard over to us. Poverty is incontestable evidence that "the family of man" is not a clever slogan but a statement about ultimate reality—the deepest reality there is about our individual lives, namely, that we belong to one another, that we need one another, that we are indissolubly bound to all God's children, and that every denial of that bond ministers only to our own destruction, just as every honoring of that bond ministers to our movement away from the edge of a terrifying abyss.

To accelerate movement away from the edge of that abyss is the seemingly impossible task of revolutionaries in the church. But it is not a hopeless task; for what Charles Reich identifies as the emergence of a new consciousness is already powerfully at work in the American psyche, profoundly affecting our common life, including the life of the churches. In *The*

Greening of America,[1] Reich illumines the church's current search for the raw materials of a new consciousness by reminding us that through the Industrial Revolution

humanity drove itself to ever higher achievements by isolating each individual and forcing him into competitive struggle. Work and culture were uprooted from the communal setting and required to serve the industrial machine. Life was regulated by a political system designed to control man's war against his fellow-man. . . . Religion, divorced from the realities of life, offered an ethical system devised to minimize the harm of the competitive and functional basis of existence without actually challenging that basis. Man harnessed himself to the machine. Beyond the industrial era lies a new age of man: the end of man's subordination to the machine and the beginning of the subjection of the machine to man—the use of technology to create a still higher level of life, based upon values that transcend the machine. . . . Man's religion and ethics will once again express a genuine community representing a balanced moral and aesthetic order. . . . In place of the childish immaturity of so many American adults, Consciousness III is developing a new independence and personal responsibility. It is seeking to replace the infantile and destructive self-seeking that we laud as "competition" by a new capacity for living and working together. . . . In Consciousness III we can see not a superficial moralistic improvement but a growth of understanding, sensibility, and the capacity for love that, for the first time, offers hope that man will be able to control and turn to good uses the machines he has built. . . . For those who were almost convinced that it was necessary to accept ugliness and evil, that it was necessary to be a miser of dreams, it is an invitation to cry or to laugh. For those who thought the world was irretrievably encased in metal and plastic and sterile stone, it seems a veritable greening of America.[2]

For the nation's churches to participate fully in that "greening of America" will be painfully difficult. Difficult for John. Difficult for Bill. Difficult for their clergy like myself. For the price of our participation in that greening is that we shall all grow up—not vaguely or generally, but quite specifically as those

---

[1] (New York: Random House, 1970).
[2] Charles A. Reich, "Reflections—The Greening of America," *The New Yorker*, September 26, 1970, pp. 42-111.

37

coming of age (see Chapter VII). However diffcult, we can take heart from the fact that the greening has indeed begun. Real hope inheres in the fact that a small but steadily growing number of business, professional, and financial leaders are caught up and are catching us up in that liberating process. These men are themselves products of the Protestant ethic, the reading of life which Reich expresses so well as "Consciousness II." A new leadership community is emerging, in Reich's telling phrase, "like flowers pushing up through a concrete pavement." [3] These "Consciousness III" people are freeing us from the prison-house of the Protestant ethic, leading us into previously unexplored dimensions of responsibility. A list of members in that company would include Catholics and Jews as well as Protestants, not only because the imprisoning myth has become truly national in scope, but also because men who escape that prison and lead us to freedom in responsibility are bound in a new fellowship which breaks down the old barriers of distinction. That emerging company would surely include men like John F. Kennedy, John Gardner, Eugene McCarthy, Charles Goodell, Arthur Goldberg, Howard Samuels, and J. Irwin Miller. In 1967 Mr. Miller, a Christian layman, was named "Businessman of the Year" by *The Saturday Review*. He is an eloquent spokesman for men come of age, and articulates a decisive dimension of a truly secular faith in Christ when he tells his fellow leaders in business:

I propose that in the judgment of future history the time is here when business should itself become "the Revolution" side—should look on itself as called by the times to become an instrument of social reform and change. . . . If, then, we ought to be reformers and revolutionists, what ought to be the character of our response to this uneasy role? To begin with, it seems clear to me that our response ought somehow to approach total response. Our concerned revolutionaries must include (along with government) education, labor, business, and the church. . . . Second, the response must be for change—and not for "going back." Third, the response must

[3] *Ibid.*

38

be not only appropriate but as rapid as the changes which create the need. We no longer have forever. We no longer have other places to which to flee. Finally, the response must be made in self-interest, never in selfish interest. . . . Our true self-interest is always best sought by seeking equally the true interest of every other man, especially those of least advantage. . . . The changes in attitude, thought, custom, and action which are now called for may well be unpredecented in history. It is not clear that we shall make them in time. If we do, it will be because we in business made accurate appraisal of what is required of us, and led the reform, the revolution, and neither opposed it, nor left it to others.[4]

Unfortunately, Mr. Miller in such an affirmation establishes himself as the exception proving the rule. He does not speak for John, nor for the overwhelming majority of Middle American laymen who are still captives of the myth and who, by and large, still control the decision-making processes in the American churches. Mr. Miller does not speak for John, in part, because the roots of John's captivity go much deeper into history than we have been able to perceive or willing to admit. Their strength goes way back through the centuries to the very beginnings of the Christian church.

Therefore we must now turn backward in time and make ourselves at once the subject and the object of a hard history lesson. It is now incumbent upon us to see that all laymen, including would-be revolutionaries like Bill, stand in John's shoes. The history lesson is not hard to understand—just hard to accept.

[4] J. Irwin Miller, quoted in "The Revolutionary Role of Business," by William D. Patterson, *The Saturday Review*, January 13, 1968, pp. 67-72.

III   History Lesson

As revolutionaries in the church we have a particular stance with regard to history. The past is crucially important to us. Not because we want to deny it or destroy it. And certainly not because we want to worship its distortions. Responsible revolutionary strategy does not assume that the goal is to dissociate ourselves from the past, or to establish ourselves independently of its built-in dynamic for change. Indeed, that dynamic is the very essence of the gospel.

We affirm the past as the wellspring of hope. We celebrate continuity rather than discontinuity precisely because history, especially the history of the people of God, is his creation, his action. History is God doing his own thing. Always, as in a mystery, he is there, in it. History matters to revolutionaries because it is perceived and experienced as the very seedbed of revolutionary impulse, the place where our roots are.

In *The Feast of Fools*, Harvey Cox affirms those roots and strengthens them by observing that

our culture in its spirited attempt to deliver us from our captivity to the past has collided with a theological problem, albeit one that few theologians recognize; how can we toast *all* the daughters of time? How can we celebrate the past, delight in the present, and gladly anticipate the future without sacrificing one to the other? The question must be asked: Does Christianity have anything to contribute to the solution of this problem? . . . The modern sensibility is correct in warning us that the past should have no favored status. It was not better, more virtuous, or closer to God. But in its crusade against the past, the modern sensibility has fallen into the snares of uncritical presentism and futurism, snares an alert theology might have helped it avoid. But theology is in no position to remove the mote from out culture's eye until it removes the beam from its own.[1]

[1] Harvey Cox, *The Feast of Fools* (Cambridge: Harvard University Press, 1969), pp. 42-43.

By way of beginning to remove that impediment to revolutionary vision, we need now to affirm continuity with the past by remembering that the Christian church did not come into being in a vacuum. It was born in, grew in, took shape in a world highly developed and organized. Part of that surrounding culture was Greek, part of it was Roman, part of it was Jewish. Inevitably, the church was always rubbing elbows with those outsiders. Much of her history is the record of what happened when Christian people came face-to-face with non-Christian ideas, persons, laws, institutions and presuppositions, all of which were, in sum, the surrounding culture.

This non-Christian environment in which Christianity grew had definite ideas, practices, and convictions about the nature and place of work in the total scheme of things. Generally speaking, that non-Christian concept rested on the notion that there were two orders of reality—a lower, inferior, material order, and a higher, superior, spiritual order. The pursuit of truth inevitably pulled one further and further away from all involvement in that lower, material, menial, physical order of things and steadily closer to the higher, spiritual realm.

Thoughtful men among the ancient Greeks disagreed on many issues, but there was a near-consensus among them on one key point, namely, that it was defiling to a man to be engaged in that lower order, demeaning to do manual labor. On this philosophical conviction about intrinsically inferior manual labor the inhuman institution of slavery rested, and from this conviction it drew its strength. Most Athenian citizens would not have been caught doing any work which obscured this distinction between the "high" and the "low." It was unworthy of their position and would have implicated them in abandonment of cherished principle. (My nineteen-year-old son reminds me wisely that this consensus was limited because there were counterculture people like Socrates around.)

Through all the early centuries of its growth, indeed through all its history, the Christian church wrestled with this idea. The most generous thing one can say is that in the resulting

41

contest of strength the Christian idea about work came off second best if, indeed, it ever really got into the fight. Throughout the Middle Ages the church took this essentially non-Christian concept of work and baptized it. Instead of rejecting that notion, as it might have, the church dressed it up in its own clothing and pretended that it had been a Christian idea all along.

The notion grew. The non-Christian concept now decked out in Christian garb informed and sustained the thought and practice of the church. The church itself became the chief cornerstone of a Medieval society which divided human beings into these same two groups—the lower mass of agricultural serfs and peasants who did the dirty, defiling work, and the higher group of nobles, aristocrats, and churchmen who believed themselves to be above such defilement and degradation.

Within the church the same basic division was made. There were two kinds of Christians, two fundamentally different categories of Christians. On the one hand there was the great mass of believers whose apprehensions of Christian truth must remain forever partial; on the other hand there was the select group, the special few, the clergy, the spiritual aristocracy, the elite, the truly religious ones whose apprehensions of truth were necessarily complete, and whose relationship to truth was necessarily authoritative. Within the church this non-Christian pattern for human society reached consummate expression in the institution of the medieval papacy; there the concept of an authoritative spiritual aristocracy became full-blown.

The result was that by the time of the Reformation very few ordinary Christian believers thought of themselves as doing any religious work. Daily work in the real world had little or no truly religious significance. Plain, ordinary men might long for God, might express that longing in worship, and did. But the clergy did the only genuinely spiritual and deeply religious work. This distinction crept into many languages spoken on the continent of Europe. To this day some Christians, in consequence of this fundamental distinction, use the word "religious" as a noun instead of an adjective: a priest, monk, or nun is referred to as "a religious," with the clear implication that the work of one outside the select, professionally religious community cannot be truly or significantly "religious" work.

This elemental cleavage between the mass of the people and the elite spiritual aristocracy was reflected even in medieval church architecture. The great cathedrals of the period were basically divided into two areas. The nave was for the great common body, the third-class passengers who were, hopefully, on their way to the celestial city, and the choir was for the dedicated community of first-class spiritual specialists. Lest there be any doubt about the distinction, the nave and the choir, in some parts of Christendom, were separated by great wooden screens, so that during vast portions of the sacred liturgy the clergy could not even be seen by the people—so pervasive was the cleavage. That wall was an incredibly accurate symbol of what was going on inside men's minds and hearts as they sought to understand their own identity.

Against that fascinating background of interlocking thought and action we can reflect creatively on one vital phase of the Protestant Reformation. What Calvin, Luther, and Knox attempted but never quite accomplished was to turn the tables on fifteen centuries of Christian history. If they bit off more than the church could chew, we should at least remember the immensity of the task to which they had set themselves. With amazing clarity, with great intellectual courage, and with a kind of gay abandon, the Reformers focused attention on the fact that what the church had done for all those centuries was to dress up the pagan notion of work in Christian clothing. They did this by demonstrating that the long-cherished distinction between the high and the low, the spiritual and the material, the sacred and the secular, that is, the distinction which created masters and slaves, nobles and serfs, *clergy and laymen*, was an utterly false distinction and, indeed, a monstrous hoax perpetrated on human society. In the redemptive providence of the Lord God, said the Reformers, that long-

43

cherished distinction on which so much of man's social, political, economic, and spiritual life has come to rest is nonexistent.

They did not stop with that negation. The Reformers went on to fill the gap they had created with a seminal insight called "the priesthood of all believers." Of course a priest has special authority, they readily granted. Of course the work of a priest has special religious significance. Of course a priest is a man set apart from the rest of men as one having a special relationship to truth. But who were the priests? As they searched the New Testament and, even more, the existential evidence of their own lives with faith and passion, they came to grips with a new answer to that decisive enquiry. That answer was: "Every man; potentially, any man." In whatever measure he lets light, love, and truth move in on him by coming to terms with the revelation in Christ, Everyman has equal access to God. In whatever measure Everyman lets that revelation make its mark upon his life he becomes and is a member of the spiritual aristocracy. Everyman, in the measure of that confrontation's reality, is an authoritative Christian specialist. Such intrepid spirits, precisely in their newly found spiritual worldliness, constitute the true and living church. Thus began the "secular" era which in our time is coming to magnificent fruition.

Thus we come to the crucial nexus. In that secular era which the Reformers began, the church was no longer primarily the priests—not because priests had been done away with but because the priesthood had opened to people in the world. In that open ministry people in the world could become profoundly authoritative guides in the quest for truth. In this context of openness, "people in the world" and "laymen doing their daily work" are synonymous. "All power to the people!"

This shining insight had one incredible implication: Whether one's daily work in the world was profoundly spiritual and significantly Christian was no longer dependent on its being a particular kind of work. "Whatever work you have to do," writes the apostle to his very unclerical friends in the church of Collossae, as he lets this reality go pulsing through his mind and heart, "do everything in the name of the Lord Jesus, put your whole heart and soul into it as into work done for God and not merely for men, since you are actually employed by Christ." He continues in the same rich vein of understanding as he writes to another group of Christian friends, in Ephesus, who had never so much as dreamed that their daily work in the world might have cosmic proportions: "You are yourselves responsible to a Heavenly Employer." In its rediscovery of the true meaning of work and thus of worldly involvement, the Reformers called upon the church, through a new understanding of the Bible, to move into a new secular age by an immense shifting of gears. And now, "after more than three centuries, we can if we will, change gears again. Our opportunity for a big step lies in opening the ministry to the ordinary Christian in much the same manner that our ancestors opened Bible reading to the ordinary Christian. To do this means in one sense the inauguration of a New Reformation, while in another it means the logical completion of the earlier Reformation in which the implications of the position taken were neither fully understood, nor loyally followed." [2]

The ministry to which all Christians are called is open. It is not a private, clerical preserve. The Christian ministry is transvocational in the sense that it stakes out its claim on all our lives and offers exciting, demanding opportunity in all work in the world. Moreover, the open ministry forces us to admit that the work of the church is not done within its own self-created and self-appointed institutional and organizational boundaries. The work of the church is done, if it is done at all, wherever men and women accept the call to the open ministry. For the church is men and women at work in the world, implementing their own priesthood, secularly and therefore in a Christian way.

This Reformation heritage of the open ministry our Protestant practice now massively denies. This unalterably secular

[2] Elton Trueblood, *Your Other Vocation* (New York: Harper & Brothers, 1952), p. 32.

45

Reformation heritage of ministry in worldliness is what we have betrayed. The result is a Protestant clericalism which makes the Roman Catholic brand about which we often fulminate mere child's play. In that department the Protestant churches are way, way ahead of whoever it is that takes second place. And so we come reluctantly into direct confrontation with the deeply disturbing question about our life together in the churches—a question so profoundly threatening both to clergy and laymen that it has become nearly unmentionable. It is a question that brings us much closer to the possibility of revolution in the church: What would it feel like to de-professionalize the Christian ministry?

IV   On De-professionalizing the Ministry

Historically, one of the accusations Protestants have consistently leveled at Roman Catholics is that the Roman church is guilty of clericalism, that is, of investing too much influence and power in the clerical hierarchy—influence and power used by clergy primarily for the aggrandizement of the church in its purely institutional identity. Clericalism thus becomes a technical or at least semitechnical term more or less synonymous with the concentration of power in a priestly class, and sometimes synonymous with abuse of that power.

Thereon hangs a sad tale of self-deception. There may be, and probably is, a Roman Catholic brand of clericalism. But there is also a Protestant brand consequent upon our practiced denial of the open ministry. Protestant clericalism is far more insidious than any Roman Catholic variety precisely because it demonstrates more clearly man's infinite capacity for self-deception. Protestant clericalism is denied by most of us clergymen. It is almost totally unrecognized, though not unfelt, by the vast majority of Protestant laymen.

This protean disease manifests itself in many ways. One of them is that Protestant laymen tend to let their reaction to the church, their feeling and conviction about the church, their participation in and support of the church be too largely determined by their purely personal reactions to the minister. The person and personality, the very being of the minister become centralized in Protestant practice because we do exactly the same thing Roman Catholics do, but in more subtle ways that seem, offhand, to be very spiritual.

Protestants thrust clergy into the center of the picture by creating certain images of the clergyman. One of those images is that of the great preacher, the pulpit genius who packs the pews week after week and whose church finally takes on not only his personality but even his very name. A sense of propriety weakens the impulse to cite obvious examples, but three seconds of thought will clarify what I mean. How many times do we hear it said of a certain church, "Oh yes, that's Dr. So-and-so's church." Such clergy, both those in charge of certain churches and those of us who are not but may secretly like to be, are the men who end professional careers with great flocks of admirers and devotees, disciples who spend sickening amounts of time helping their heroes adjust self-constructed halos. The less we say about this particular heresy the kinder we shall be to some of the leading clerical religionists of our time.

Another image strengthening the hold of clericalism is that of the clergyman as local saint, the "man of God," the moral example, the one on whom supposedly the citizenry in general and young people in particular can pattern their lives. This image implies what is demonstrably untrue, namely, that the clergyman is by virtue of training, ordination, and other unspecified processes closer to God and therefore more "spiritual" than a layman. If, by some uncalculated revelation of his humanity, it becomes apparent that he is not more spiritual, the image is nevertheless maintained by the clear lay conviction that he ought to be. In either instance, the power of Protestant clericalism grows.

It needs firmly to be said that laymen are not the only ones who play this deadly game. Clergy play it, too. We participate for the simple, sufficient reason that playing the game sustains the ego, especially if the ego-structure is frail, hurt, shrunken, or possessed by basically unresolved personal or vocational anxieties. Our participation is a way of playing with fire. Even primitives understood fire to be one of the primordial elements. Primitive men pursued fire, felt fire, desired fire, and worshiped fire not only for its light and heat, but also for its intrinsic mystical fascinations. Clergy know those fascinations never cease. So we sometimes enter this fatal game in the manner of little boys playing with matches, but more often, I think, in the subtly sophisticated manner of primitives, for whom the worship of fire is a compulsive quest for certainty in an uncertain universe whose mysteries often leave us feeling alienated, threatened, alone.

Be that as it may, the game is a disease. It infects us clergy. It infects laymen. It debilitates the body of Protestant life, thought, and action. In briefest compass, I shall list just a few of the consequences.

1. Clericalism, because it preserves a false distinction between clergy and laymen, keeps clergy from knowing who we are. If clergy tend, as we do, to be pompous, stuffy, dull, cheaply pious and, what is worse than all these, strangers to ourselves, it is in large part because the coexistence of clericalism and honesty, in one psyche, is not a live option.

2. Clericalism militates against communication between clergy and laymen because it feeds on a complex of images not rooted in the realities of our human life and nature. Clericalism nourishes pretense, unreality, artificiality, and phoniness in the relationship of clergy and laymen because it feeds on a lie about who clergy are and what we are like.

3. Clericalism emasculates worship because it tends to make the value of worship dependent on the allegedly superior spirituality of clergy. It also emasculates worship because it tends to remove laymen from genuine participation in worship; it conceals from laymen the truth that worship is common worship, the activity, action, and response of the believing community, a community in which the clergyman is only one among many members.

4. Clericalism makes laymen too content with their biblical illiteracy because it tends to make clergy the sole dividers and dispensers of the Word of God. In so doing, clericalism relieves the layman of any real conviction that it is exactly his, the layman's, responsibility to search out and be searched by the living Word in Scripture.

5. Clericalism paralyzes the ethical muscles of the church by implying that it is the business of clergy to make Christian

49

witness in the world, and to do this in behalf of laymen, always of course with the proviso that it be done noncontroversially and with a minimum of fuss. After all, we are paid to do it. We are not paid very well, as such things go, but we are paid. The monthly paycheck has subtly and pervasively become a symbol, a largely unrecognized, largely unconscious but for that very reason potent symbol of clerical professionalism. I speak now of a dimension of professionalism which is equally the sin of laymen and clergy, because it represents the willingness of both to play this deadly game, a game which makes Christian witness in the world the work of a few specialists who devote themselves to what we euphemistically call "full-time Christian service." In the history of American Protestantism, that saccharine phrase has helped produce a whole army of laymen who have been quite content to be part-time Christian workers with no pressing sense of genuine responsibility in and for the coming of the kingdom of God in the world. Thus does clericalism reduce the acceptance of responsibility for the growth of that Kingdom in the hearts of men, and in the structures by which men order their common lives. However deadly for the church and unredemptive for the world, clericalism is a game which rewards all participants, lay and clergy.

6. Clericalism aggravates and intensifies the temptation of the church as institution to become the latest evidence for the validity of C. N. Parkinson's Law. The growing tendency of the Protestant church to become a ponderously monstrous, parkinsonian bureaucracy feeding upon itself, rather than a redeeming fellowship at work in the world, is the consequence of clericalism's assigning the "real" work of the church to professionals while giving to the Kingdom's second- and third-class citizens—laymen—the leftover busy work, and the dubious privilege of paying the bills.

7. Clericalism makes man the measure of all things in the church, not God-in-Christ. It centralizes man, secondarily represented by laymen, primarily represented by the superior crea-

tures who are the clergy. Such is the decline and fall into which clericalism leads the church.

Our Protestant clericalism is a huge, insidious lie which preserves and nourishes the false philosophical distinction between spirit and matter, the false medieval economic distinction between nobleman and serf, the false cultural distinction between sacred and secular, the false political distinction between ruler and ruled, the false religious distinction between holiness and worldliness. For all these reasons the big lie has become a plague in the Protestant churches, a principal impediment to revolution.

The most tragic result of that plague has been implicit in all that has gone before; now it must be made explicit. That tragedy is the fact that the true name of the game called clericalism is: "Let's Waste Laymen." That is what we are doing. So far as the church in the world is concerned, laymen are being wasted on an immense scale. Their intelligence is being wasted, their education and training are being wasted, their desire to make their lives count is being wasted, their knowledge of the world is being wasted. Of course there are, thank God, notable and obvious exceptions. But they are exceptions to the rule, the rule being that our professional clericalism and our clerical professionalism undermine, distort, devalue, denigrate, and in many instances totally destroy their God-given ministry in the world. Clericalism does this by a combination of refusal and denial with regard to one largely unrecognized but infinitely important fact: that in the world laymen are the best ministers, indeed, in most of that endlessly intriguing mystery which is the world laymen are the only ministers the church has.

The point may be clarified by thinking of the criticism which many laymen, especially laymen like John, level against many clergy because of their growing tendency to get involved in social, economic, and political matters. As we all know, this has been especially true in the racial crisis. How many laymen like John have said of the involved clergyman, "Why doesn't he

51

stay home and act like a minister?" Or, "Why doesn't he tend to his own business in the church?" About such remarks a couple of things need to be said. One is that whatever happens in any community to make men hurt is precisely the business of Christian ministers. Another is that laymen should be on their knees thanking God for every clergyman who cares sufficiently about people to involve himself in the personal, corporate, structural, and systemic causes of their pain.

This is not to say that we clergymen should be free of criticism on the matter of involvement in large social problems. On the contrary, we should be criticized, but for quite a different reason. The tragic flaw in contemporary Christian witness is not that so many clergymen are mixed up in political, social, and economic questions, not that so many clergymen are involved in problems relating directly to jobs or housing or schools or to the power structures where decisions are made for those decisive areas of our common life. Not at all. The tragic flaw in contemporary Christian witness is that so few laymen are entering those arenas of human need. If clergy are the proper objects of criticism by laymen, it ought to be for our failure to help laymen get deeply and inextricably "mixed up," as Christians, in the great issues, problems, and agonies of our public life. Clergy should be criticized not because our involvement in those struggles is wrong but rather because, held in the grips of rabid clericalism, we have tried to make our personal involvement a substitute for lay involvement in those scenes of God's action.

I learned to make that crucial distinction three years ago through the involvement of Central Church in a community enterprise called the Lackawanna Plaza Urban Renewal Project. In Montclair, which is a New York City suburb of forty-five thousand, the Lackawanna Plaza area is an ugly sore on the municipal face. Led by Union Baptist Church, the churches of the community were confronted with an opportunity to form a nonprofit corporation whose purpose would be to heal that sore by building and managing several million dollars worth of relocation housing in the area. Union Development Corporation thus came into being for the purpose of making the whole area a more human place to live.

For Central Church the toughest questions included these: shall we be involved at all? Shall we be a cosponsor of the corporation? Shall we contribute money? How much? Isn't housing the work of other agencies in town? Why does the church get mixed up in such a nonreligious problem? How can we justify the expenditures of church monies for such a project? Isn't this getting the church into politics? What about our members who don't believe the church as a corporate body should be involved in public issues? Isn't housing a matter for experts? Won't this take away money from other projects already established by the national boards and agencies of our church?

To seek answers to these and many other questions, our official board, the Session, created what was called "The Lackawanna Plaza Project Committee." The final outcome was that Central Church did become one of the founders of the corporation, did contribute a substantial sum of money, did get involved, and our efforts along with those of many others are now bearing final fruit. The redevelopment of the Lackawanna Plaza area is about to begin, and it will be a more human environment. But that fact, important as it is, is not what I want to focus on here. Rather it is important to zero in on what we, as a church, learned in and through the whole experience.

That importance rests not with the technical details of the Lackawanna Plaza Project, but rather with the process through which we developed a viable model for the future, a model that has wide applicability to all sorts of opportunities for Christian witness. The steps in that process were as follows:

1. A need became apparent. In this case, the need happened to be for better housing in the most blighted area in our community.

2. A group of people gathered around that need. In this

case, the gathered group happened to be The Lackawanna Plaza Project Committee.

3. The gathered group addressed itself to a specific question: Should our Christian faith involve us in a response to this need, and is there a way in which we could join our fellow-Christians in the church in such a response? Because their work was limited to this task, it was clear that they were, in a strict sense, a "task force."

4. The task force embraced the disciplines inherent in the complexities of an urban society. In this instance they became sophisticated and expert in a very intricate facet of that complexity, namely, housing. This required hard work, many hours, the willingness to master new knowledge, and a readiness to change their minds.

5. As a result of the preceding four steps the task force discerned, in a particular area of human life and enterprise, the secular content of the gospel of Christ. In a purely secular commitment, Christ's lordship was celebrated.

6. The task force then proceeded to share the fruits of their discipline with other responsible groups of their fellow-Christians, namely, the Session, the trustees, and the congregation, thus creating for a whole group of Christians (Central Presbyterian Church) an opportunity for growth in their own lives as individuals and in their life together as the Body of Christ.

7. Most importantly, the task force, through its embrace of a secular discipline, demonstrated that in a complex, technologically oriented, urban society it is only laymen who can be the church. The clergy were present in this whole process, but they were peripheral. The work was done, the insights were developed, the disciplines were embraced by laymen. Through the task force, power was placed in the hands of laymen (Session, trustees, congregation).

I have described in some detail this single experience centering around Lackawanna Plaza because it illumines an ultimate, utterly crucial insight: The only healing there is, or can be, for that clericalism which infests Protestant witness and vitiates Protestant mission, inheres in a totally new understanding of Christian ministry. Whether that understanding is called "the open ministry" or however else it is labeled, that understanding must be one which recognizes laymen, accepts laymen, trains laymen, and deploys laymen as those who are always the best and often the only ministers the church has in the world. "This shift in the character of ministry," writes Gibson Winter, "can be dramatized thus: the ministry is usually conceived today as the work of clergymen with auxiliary aids among the laity; ministry in the servant Church is the work of laity in the world with auxiliary help from theological specialists." [1]

Is it not ironic that most of us learned to say, "God so loved the world that he gave his only Son," and, "God sent the Son into the world not to condemn the world, but that the world might be saved through him," almost as soon as we could talk, and that we have been repeating such words off and on ever since without getting the faintest glimmer of what they imply about the nature of ministry? What manifestly escaped us or, more accurately, what we have tried to escape is God's love affair with the world, an affair whose consequence is his identification with the world, his real Presence in the world.

Where is that world? That divinely loved, ultimately affirmed world is wherever laymen live, labor, plan, act, influence, decide, fail, and triumph whenever they are not sharing in the gathered life of the church. It is there, primarily, in the midst of whatever secular strivings have already engaged laymen, there that they will feel the divine Presence, if ever they do there that laymen will know the divine Power if ever they do, there that laymen will do the divine Will, if ever they do, for the world is God's Holy of Holies. Translated, this simply means that he is more fully alive and present in the human needs of the Lackawanna Plaza area than he is in the sanctuary

---

[1] Gibson Winter, *The New Creation as Metropolis* (New York: The Macmillan Company, 1963), p. 59.

of Central Church, and that laymen are therefore best equipped to lead us in the discernment and practice of that Presence.

Such is the insight which brings us to a primary mark of the de-professionalized, de-clericalized servant church. In the first instance that kind of church is a group of concerned, committed laymen who, precisely because of their secular involvements have decisive clues concerning the whereabouts of God. This is not to suggest that the lay-oriented church we must become shall have no gathered life. But it does clearly mean that when the members of the church come together in any aspect of our gathered life, we do not do so in order to retreat or withdraw or escape from the world. When the church gathers, it is still in the world, and it gathers, that is, *we* gather, for worship or study or prayer or sacrament for the world's sake. Whatever we do together in the church has justification solely in the measure that it prepares laymen for ministry in the world. If anything we do in the gathered life of the church does not so fortify, strengthen, and prepare laymen, then it is at best an irrelevance and, at worst, an abomination, a curse, a malignancy in the Body of Christ.

Because the de-professionalized servant church leans on laymen who seek, find, love, serve, and know God in the world, it is also a church willing to let the world write its agenda. This does not mean that the church has no built-in sensors with which to direct its life, so that it is pushed around aimlessly by whatever happens to be going on around it. But it does mean that those sensors are buried deeply in the most baffling complexes of secular reality, and that they are tuned to give the church first-hand data about whatever it is in such reality that makes any of God's children wince with pain. Structure and organization must develop in response to the felt pain of the world. Agenda-formation becomes a very risky business, for there is the obvious built-in chance that such a church may get the wrong signals or no signals at all. Nevertheless, the de-professionalized servant church must organize itself around, and address itself to, the world's cries for help and meaning, relying for leadership primarily on laymen sufficiently sophisticated, empathetic, and dedicated to understand that those cries are the voice of a sovereign Lord in whose service is the raw material of their own maturity and the rationale of their own lives.

Such is the import and essential thrust of the profoundly gripping moment in the seventh chapter of Luke when John sends two of his disciples to Jesus to ask him whether he, Jesus, really is God, or whether he, John, should look elsewhere. In response to this inquiry about the reality of his authority and the validity of his claims, questioned at that ultimate level where the whole Christian reading of life stands or falls, lives or dies, has reality and is reality or else is nothing and less than nothing, Jesus merely says to John's disciples: Take a look at the world and at what is happening there. Then, "Go and tell John what you have seen and heard: the blind receive their sight, the lame walk, lepers are cleansed, and the deaf hear, the dead are raised up, the poor have good news preached to them. And blessed is he who takes no offense at me." The world's pain writes the agenda for the church because it is in response to that pain of the world that the church follows its Lord and represents him, fulfilling its ministry through laymen. How those laymen can be identified, gathered, trained, and disciplined is a revolutionary question of great strategic importance which will be discussed later. In the meantime, it behooves us to strip our minds for action by grasping the sense in which most of our organized activities, programs, services, committees, boards, and procedures in the church are properly identified as "heretical structures." Why? Because so much of our church organization, activity, and even worship actually prevents laymen from being and becoming the servant church in God's world. Not directly and aggressively and with irreligious passion. Not at all. The whole thing is really quite subtle. Our institutional realities and priorities are heretical because with them and through them we deceive ourselves about the true nature of the church, the true significance of

57

the world, and the inviolability of their interrelatedness. Much of what now passes for church worship or activity is heretical because it drains away the good and precious energy of laymen and leaves them vaguely feeling, if not deeply believing, that they have somehow been engaged in a "good" thing. If there ever was a time when the church could get by with such prodigal wasting of lay resources, that time is gone. We simply cannot afford any longer to play "let's waste laymen." Not when a whole world—God's world, a world he inhabits, a world where he awaits our company—is crying out for the ministry of a servant church, a de-professionalized ministry which laymen can best fulfill.

If we were to take this concept of open ministry in a de-professionalized church seriously, think what a difference it would make! Ponder the revolution it would produce in our worship. Gaze into the ludicrous, ridiculous, tragicomic light it would throw on much of what we now call "church" activity. Contemplate the deliverance from nonparticipatory and spectator attitudes it would bring. Feel for the depths of biblical study into which it would force us. Savor the excitement it would rouse in our hearts and minds. Calculate, if you can, the opposition and resistance it would arouse because of our instinctive hatred for all deep-seated change. Speculate about the creative involvement and demanding dialogue with the problems and struggles of the secular city in which it would place us. Measure the dignity and glory it would bring to the word "member," for membership would then be a thing of intrinsic greatness. Think of the maturation of minds and hearts it would produce. Ponder the deepened sense of responsibility it would create among us—felt, honored, accepted responsibility—responsibility for schools and housing and jobs and juvenile delinquency, responsibility for justice in our society. Consider the new relationships it would establish among the arts, the sciences, the business enterprises of the city, and the church. Think of the leverage it would create on seemingly immovable objects and allegedly irresistible forces of decay and dissolution. Feel your way into the engagements, in some instances the mortal combats, with the prevailing culture it would provoke. Think of the newness, the freshness, the vigor of mind it would produce as laymen began to bear the burden of religious teaching and theological reflection consequent upon their discernments of God at work in the midst of the human struggle.

That brings me to George and Ken, two real, live laymen in Central Church, Montclair. (Again, as with John and Bill, I have given these two men different names, not to conceal their identity but to save them embarrassment as I describe the magnificent things happening in their lives and make bold to identify them as living examples of the kind of laymen I am writing about.)

George grew up in Montclair and has for years been at the heart of its leadership community. He is keenly intelligent, affable, and always involved in all sorts of good, civic projects around town. He is president of a manufacturing company which employs several hundred black and brown workers from metropolitan Newark. About two years ago the Session of Central Church, in response to the concern of one of its members, and several other laymen organized and sponsored a three-day interracial confrontation. About thirty men and women, black and white, most but not all of whom were members of Central Church, spent a weekend together in a YMCA Conference Center in Pawling, New York.

George decided to go because he felt it important for him to increase his communications skills as chairman of the town's redevelopment agency. In that role he had become significantly related to the black community because of the redevelopment project in Lackawanna Plaza, described earlier.

The Pawling experience turned out to be decisive in George's life. So decisive that I shall later identify its relationship to what the church has traditionally called "salvation" and "evangelism." For the purposes of the present context, however, all I wish to affirm is that Pawling was a totally secular experience in the sense that there was no discussion of God or religion or the Bible, but only a grass-roots exploration of why there was so little black-white understanding in Montclair, and this in the nitty-gritty context of our own lives and feelings. As a result of that secular immersion, George returned to Montclair —to this community, to his home, to his company, and to his church—a changed man.

I do not mean that he suddenly got "religion" in any traditional sense. I do mean that his confrontation with a very real slice of felt pain and struggle in the secular world produced fundamental alteration in his reality perceptions, so that he became in very truth a new kind of leader in the world and in the church. The revolutionary community of lay leaders in a de-professionalized servant church is really emerging.

Another example is Ken who is a lawyer and a businessman. Throughout most of his adult life, Ken found himself in a state of creative disaffiliation from the church—not opposed to it but certainly not energized by it. As a lawyer Ken moved closer and closer to the business community and eventually became an owner and principal manager of a significant enterprise in the financial industry. But all through the years of his involvement in business, he sustained an active interest in the scholarly and academic dimensions of the law.

About four years ago he started coming to Central Church. Seldom did he miss a Sunday. Week after week he heard a consistent attempt to discern the presence of God in the midst of the most desperate crises of our times—race, poverty, war, automation, the student rebellion, the insensitivity of the establishment. During all this time Ken was himself passing through a vocational crisis in the sense that his success in the legal profession as a practicing lawyer and in the financial industry as an executive no longer fulfilled him. He was longing and searching for something more—something that would add new dimensions of meaning to his life, giving it the feeling of more genuine relationship to the kind of responsibility he was all the time hearing about in church.

Not quickly or easily, but over a period of many months Ken finally decided to leave Montclair and New York and accept the invitation to become a professor of law in the law school of a large eastern university. He made this decision for many reasons. One is that he now perceives a great need, as a corporation lawyer, to develop and train a whole new breed of young corporation lawyers who will be concerned at unprecedented levels to establish new relationships between corporate responsibility and the social crisis. Indeed, those words, "Corporate Responsibility and the Social Crisis," constitute the title of a definitive article Ken has written and published in his school's Law Review since taking up his professorial duties. In his own words, it is an article which seeks "to collect and analyze all the relevant, judicial, administrative, and statutory materials in an effort to understand the development of the standards of corporate responsibility in the past, and to determine the present scope of legal authority for business participation in the solution of the critical social problems of our times."

The point I want to make is that those words describe not just the thrust of one article in a Law Review. They have also become the professional purpose of Ken's whole life. And this purpose—the training of young lawyers in the meaning of social responsibility—by Ken's own testimony happened decisively because of Central Church. He has left Central Church, but he is in very truth a minister in that law school, "doing his thing" in the de-professionalized servant church, serving God secularly by teaching a new breed of lawyers how to make life more human for the whole family of man. When Ken sent me a reprint of his article on corporate responsibility and the social crisis, he penned a statement which indicates that the weekly bath in secularity which he received at Central Church was what made all the difference. I shall examine that difference in the next chapter.

For now, it is sufficient to affirm that the revolutionary community of lay leaders in a de-professionalized servant church is indeed emerging. Such auspicious possibilities as those raised by George and Ken are the raw material of revolution in the church. Let them be a reminder to all laymen that the whole meaning of their lives, not just as churchmen but also as human beings, is now bound up with becoming the creators of this proposed revolution. Everything is at stake, as George and Ken both testify about their lives. Their experience should make us all aware that we are now dealing with a matter as basic and fundamental as any. For their experience raises the question about the inmost identity of laymen.

When Jesus says, "you are the salt of the earth," it is not just a nice, gently suggestive oriental metaphor. Rather, it is an uncompromising assertion laying bare the very meaning and purpose of human life in this world. All Christians, of course, but especially Christian laymen must be sensitive to the inflexibly nonpermissive quality of Christ's mind at this point, for he speaks especially to laymen about the meaning of salt. He does not say: Do you believe that you are the salt of the earth? or, Would you like to be the salt of the earth? He says neither that you ought to be the salt of the earth, nor that you have the salt of the earth, but quite simply and directly that you *are* the salt of the earth. Bonhoeffer makes this illuminating comment: "It is not for the disciples to decide whether they will be the salt of the earth, for they are so whether they like it or not, they have been made salt by the call they have received. . . . The word [about salt] speaks of their whole existence in so far as it is grounded anew in the call of Christ." [2]

Before laymen accept or reject the invitation to participate in a revolution, let them be sure of this: The invitation is rooted not in some humanistic estimate of their potential,

[2] Dietrich Bonhoeffer, *The Cost of Discipleship* (New York: The Macmillan Company, 1953), p. 100 (Macmillan Paperbacks Edition [1963], p. 130).

not in some frail restructuring of the church's corporate life, not in some shallow reorientation of liturgical or theological or ethical emphases, but rather in Christ's own reading of their magnificently manifest destiny in the ongoing processes of history. To affirm that laymen are the salt of the earth is his own sovereign way of saying that the processes of historical decay shall be arrested through their ministries in the world. But beyond that, so also shall the healing, redemptive processes of restoration and renewal be initiated and brought to fruition by their ministries in the world. What the church needs, what the world needs, what laymen who are the church in the world need is to be renewed by the discovery or rediscovery of their mission in life, their reason for being.

The justification of their existence and the rationale for their whole life must be found in acceptance of personal responsibility for the making and molding of history. That acceptance of responsibility can be made only in the world where laymen live, move, and have their being, the world in which they are called to ministry by the voice of one who speaks of the oppressed, the lonely, the sick, the imprisoned, the victims of injustice and prejudice and discrimination, along with the equally tragic victims of those dehumanizing forces at work among the affluent and the successful, and says of them *all*, inasmuch as you do it unto one of the least of these my brethren, you do it unto me, for I am with them, there in the world, waiting for you to join me in making their lives whole. There, in the flowing and ebbing tides of history, there in the midst of whatever it is that makes men suffer, there in the agonies and ecstasies of metropolis, in the maelstrom of war, in the whirling cesspool of a culture gone mad; there in the midst of every stricken people's revolution of rising expectations, in the baffling mazes of technology and space, in classrooms and city slums and executive suites and country clubs— wherever laymen are in the world shall they find salvation. For the world is where God is.

Laymen are now confronted with one of the greatest opportunities in all Christian history. Theirs is the chance to rebuild the church by de-professionalizing it and making the church worldly. Worldly not in the sense that the church is now shaped and shackled by that which is worn out and passing away. Rather, the worldliness which laymen are called to create in the church is the kind Bonhoeffer meant when he wrote from his prison cell:

I don't mean the shallow this-worldliness of the enlightened, of the busy, the comfortable or the lascivious. It's something much more profound than that, something in which the knowledge of death and resurrection is ever present. . . . It is only by living completely in this world that one learns to believe. . . . It is in such a life that we throw ourselves utterly in the arms of God and participate in his sufferings in the world and watch with Christ in Gethsemane. That is faith, that is *metanoia* [repentance], and that is what makes a man and a Christian. . . . How can success make us arrogant or failure lead us astray, when we participate in the sufferings of God by living in this world? [3]

Robert Clyde Johnson comments on Bonhoeffer's truly seminal contribution to our understanding of the worldliness to which God is calling the church and in so doing makes one of his own: "By definition, the Christian is not one who turns his back upon—or even one who intermittently turns aside from—the world. The Christian is not one who seeks a means of escape from the brutal realities of life, nor is he one who yearns nostalgically for some haven of serenity and security outside of, or above, the overpowering tides of history. No, by definition, the Christian is one who stands in the midst of the world to minister to the world. He is the one who seeks, beyond all else, to be an instrument of the redemptive mission of the worldly God, the God who gave Himself to the world, and for the world, the God whom we know

[3] Dietrich Bonhoeffer, *Letters and Papers from Prison* (New York: Macmillan Paperbacks Edition, 1962), pp. 225-26.

because he has stood alongside us in the world, shared our lot, and thus transformed it." [4]

The holy, open, de-professionalized ministry of a *worldly* church is calling laymen. Worldy through its response to the tensions and tragedies of history. Worldly in the truly magnificent sense that it makes men responsible in history and for history. Worldly in the sense that the church makes man truly human. To hear that call and accept it will be more difficult for most people in our present churches than it was for Bonhoeffer, even though he suffered and died in a Nazi concentration camp. In many ways it has always been easier for the church to be Christian in circumstances of obvious crisis, where it does not have around its neck so much dead weight of custom and tradition. The task is not simple, nor will any man help by proposing simplistic solutions.

But we must act. For "if salt loses its saltness, it is good for nothing but to be thrown out and trodden under foot by men." That means that it is not only salvation, but also judgment which emerges as a live option for men whose moral and spiritual freedom is the real article. And ours is. Being the very image in which we are created, our freedom includes the freedom to reject our own destiny. This staggering, awesome possibility, writes Bonhoeffer with consummate wisdom, "is the judgement which always hangs over the disciple community, whose mission is to save the world, but which, if it ceases to live up to that mission, is itself irretrievably lost. The call of Jesus Christ means either that we are the salt of the earth, or else we are annihilated; either we follow the call or we are crushed beneath it." [5]

Faced with such alternatives we must grope through unyielding darkness toward light which may or may not be there at the end of our long, dark tunnel. That movement from

[4] Robert C. Johnson, ed., "The Church and Its Changing Ministry," The General Assembly of the United Presbyterian Church in the U.S.A. (Philadelphia), p. 11.
[5] *The Cost of Discipleship*, p. 100 (Paperbacks Edition, p. 131).

65

darkness to light will occur in our lives and in the life of the church only if we dismantle and reconstruct our present understanding of two fundamental matters. We shall attempt this dismantling and reconstruction remembering that a truly radical crisis such as the present one in the church requires truly radical remedies. But radical remedies are never healing unless they are also responsible. We must set off in quest of a truly liberating insight.

V   The Liberating Insight

In the past it has been the general habit and conviction of most Christians to insist that our Lord and Savior Christ can be known and is known in a human vacuum. According to this time-honored view—held, I should think, in some degree by the vast majority of Christians in the world today—belief in God and commitment to Christ are primal acts of the mind and heart, followed automatically and inevitably by acts of brotherhood and responsibility in the human community. In this view, knowledge of God, confrontation with God, and personal relation to God are all highly "spiritual" experiences which can and do occur in man's aloneness with his Creator and Lord.

The characteristic milieu for this alleged encounter is a whole complex of arrangements, activities, priorities, and disciplines which includes certain aspects of study, worship, prayer, and, in some Christian circles, what is called "giving your life to Christ." So far as human beings are concerned this characteristic environment for the encounter does not really include them, except as they become props for the setting of the play. They are not really members of the cast.

It is all very "spiritual," and the church has built upon the base of this alleged spirituality a whole theology of something called Christian experience. With regard to human beings in their complex, interweaving relationships to one another, that is, with regard to changing the structures by which men order their common lives, this time-honored theology says in essence: Change men by having them know God-in-Christ, and these changed men will in turn change human society for the better. The clearly implied sequence is: First the encounter with Christ. After that, the changed order of relationship to human beings and institutions.

My purpose is not to throw out the baby with the bath by dismissing as totally erroneous a whole, highly developed, and firmly embraced body of conviction held by so many people. Nor would any responsible person deny that Christians who hold these views have had productive and responsible relationships to their fellow human beings. Of course they have. But it is my clear intention on the basis of evidence to call in question the basic validity of their primary assumptions concerning the whereabouts of God and the locale of the divine-human encounter. Where is that evidence?

That evidence is in such biblical passages as Matthew 25 where we are clearly told of God's presence in the need of our neighbor. That evidence is in the biblical doctrine of creation, where we are reminded that it is not church or doctrine or dogma, but the world itself that the Creator inhabits. It is in the biblical doctrine of Incarnation, which confronts us with God's presence not only in Christ as Man, but in man as Man. It inheres in the fact that the forces of renewal and restoration in our human society come quite as much from non-Christians as they do from Christians of this time-honored persuasion. It inheres in the fact that Christians who stand solidly behind this traditional position do not really possess any deeper existential knowledge of God than the rest of us, nor any significantly more responsible human relationships than those of us who seek a new faith for a new day.

If we take all these complex factors into balanced consideration, it becomes legitimate and honest and responsible to wonder and to ask out loud whether the church has managed to perpetrate a gigantic hoax upon itself and most of its members. A hoax in which the thing it calls "knowledge of God" is not so much knowledge of God as it is familiarity with its own long-established distortions of truth, not so much knowledge of God as it is conformity to the limitations of its own courage.

"The fundamental quality of all human relationships," writes Otto Piper in his book A *Christian Interpretation of Sex*, is found in the fact that I have to do with Christ Himself in my dealings with every other person. Whenever I meet another person it is Christ who offers me a possibility of finding Himself in that person. That other person is, in this way, in a position to transform my natural being into that of a child of God. . . . Wherever I may be . . . God approaches me, and whoever may come into contact with me . . . is, therefore, my neighbor, that is, the very person whom I need. The truth is that when Christ helps us encounter another person, an invaluable gift is made to us through that other person. And everything depends on our accepting this gift. It is belief in the presence of Christ in the other person that gives rise to genuine fellowship in spite of natural differences. . . . I would despise God's gift if I did not deal with him as with Christ Himself.[1]

This essential insight about meeting, discerning, and knowing Christ in the context of all human relationships could remind us, if we wanted and permitted it to, that it was not just the human life of Jesus of Nazareth that God made wholly his own. Incarnation means that it was and is *all* human life to which he indissolubly binds himself. Incarnation means, as we have traditionally surmised, that God was in Christ reconciling the world to himself. But it also means, as we have perhaps surmised but have been unwilling to admit, that God-in-Christ was and is in Man himself. Not man alone. Not man in isolation. Not man embracing the monastic solution of separation from his fellows, but man in relationship to man: There God-in-Christ is found, located, known, worshiped, served, loved. In human communion, in society where man meets and deals with, affects and is affected by, his fellowman, there does the divine-human encounter occur or fail to occur.

If we are to speak with integrity of that encounter and care about the encounter between God and man, if it does matter that man and God shall have something personal to do with each other, then we must keep the discussion of such encounter and the attempt to nourish it in the exact context

[1] Otto Piper, A *Christian Interpretation of Sex* (New York: Charles Scribner's Sons, 1941), pp. 108-10.

where Jesus himself placed it, namely, in the relationship of man to man. Such loyalty to Jesus is neither flabbly immanentism nor shallow humanism. Rather, it is an exalted and infinitely responsible view of personal Christian salvation. It is a deliberate and considered abandonment of all pious efforts to deny that personal saving knowledge of God comes to us in the relationships of our human society. It is a biblically rooted, doctrinally sound, and existentially verified affirmation that individual, saving, divine-human encounter comes through personal involvement in the restoration of the human community.

Clearly the time has come in the history of the church for the emerging revolutionary community on whom its future depends to affirm, confidently and joyously, the first dimension of the liberating insight: The church must break outside its own institutional, organizational, structural, liturgical, and theological ghettos and be found in identity with the world of men and of their human needs, not in order to do good, not in order to implement a social vision, but precisely in order to find, meet, and know God-in-Christ. The time has come in the history of the church when those of us who are criticized for wanting to get the church mixed up in social problems at the expense of what has traditionally been called "inner spiritual reality" must turn to our critics and meet them on their own ground by saying: "Yes, it is precisely personal salvation that we are talking about when we advocate deep, radical, corporate, and personal involvements in the world of human need. Just like you and with you, what we are talking about is that age-old question, Where does a man meet God and really know him?" In a time when some are saying that the church must not be involved in social problems because the principal business of the church is with the "spiritual" part of life, some Christians are surely being called by the living God to reply by saying: "Yes, we do want the church to be involved in those problems on a scale of massively sophisticated responsibility to the end that the members of the church may confront and be confronted by their Lord and Savior Christ."

I contend that that saving confrontation is exactly what has happened in the lives of George and Ken about whom I wrote in the preceding chapter. For George, salvation emerged as a live option in the context of that probing, agonized, fully human, totally secular interracial confrontation which I have already described. During that crucial weekend at Pawling the name of Christ was never mentioned, perhaps not even thought of. But that power of Christ which is so sovereign as to invite anonymity was surely felt and known in George's life. That whole episode was salvational for him, precisely because the confrontation was so uncompromisingly secular, so human, so totally given to the search for understanding, healing, and restoration, as those experiences are humanly comprehended and humanly informed. It was in the searing context of his own and others' fiercely affirmed humanity that George knew deity—sovereignly secular Christian deity.

For Ken, the data were different, but the insight which the data illumined was the same. Over a long period of months Ken's essential search was for felt relationship between the humanly oriented issues raised persistently in church and the meaning of his own life. The longing to make his life a more adequate servant of social justice and responsibility was not experienced by Ken as anything particularly religious or spiritual. On the contrary, it was experienced by him as a thorough going, secular, vocational reorientation. As such, he perceived its ingredients in very human terms and categories—students, businessmen, corporations, careers, issues, etc. And for that same reason—its earthiness, its this-worldliness, its secularity, its humanness—it was an experience and growing knowledge of the sovereign Lord who uses that secularity and humanness as the raw material of his salvational confrontations with man. The word "salvation" is probably not yet in Ken's working vocabulary, but it doesn't need to be there because the dynam-

71

ic power of the salvation experience is there in Ken's life, known and appropriated through his ever-deepening involvements in the restoration of human community. Indeed, the salvation-confrontation is so deep and true in his life that Ken, while he resided in Montclair, was not even a member of the church. Ken's very integrity made that step impossible, and the sovereignty of the saving Christ made it unnecessary, because true sovereignty is unlimited enough to be Most Deeply Experienced in human secularity.

In Ken's life, and in George's, the reality of the salvation experience is verified, as it must now be verified in all our lives, by the measure in which they are willing to tolerate personal disturbance. In understanding salvation as an essentially secular, human experience, we must learn to identify and accept disturbance as a new theological category. George and Ken experienced salvation secularly because they were willing, on a sustained and truly personal basis, to be disturbed, disturbed by their no-holds-barred struggle with questions every Christian must now learn to make his own. The saving-disturbing questions will vary with individuals, but for each one of us the catalog of disturbances will surely include inquiries like these:

Am I willing to be disturbed by admitting that most of the religious-sounding things which I say I believe, I don't really believe at all?

Am I willing to be disturbed by admitting that most of what I say I believe is so phony, so lacking in authenticity, that I haven't even been able effectively to communicate it to my own children, to say nothing of getting them to feel within themselves that it might be true?

Am I willing to be disturbed by facing honestly the probability that what I am pleased euphemistically to call my Christian life has confused, discouraged, and hurt at least as many people as it has helped, and perhaps more?

Am I willing to be disturbed by openly admitting, not to

72

others but to myself, the yawning chasm between what I profess and what I do?

Am I willing to be disturbed by getting to know persons utterly different from myself? By reading and studying books which express ideas and convictions utterly different from my own? By plunging myself into human and institutional situations in ways that may, and probably will, offend the guardians of the status quo? By listening carefully and respectfully to people who disagree with me?

Am I willing to be disturbed by admitting, not to others but to myself, that I have used the church to shield me not only from costly involvement in the crying needs of the world, but also from committed enjoyment of its excitements and its opportunities?

Am I willing to be disturbed by admitting that I have not studied significantly in the field of religion or faith since I picked up a few childhood notions about the Bible twenty, thirty, or forty years ago?

Am I willing to be disturbed by honoring those prophets in our society who challenge, question, and threaten everything for which I have stood, everything I have held sacred, everything I have so piously identified with Christian faith and life?

Am I willing to be disturbed by admitting my own personal role in and responsibility for the present institutional paralysis of the church?

Am I willing to be disturbed by some of my fellow-Christians who would like nothing more than to see the church turned upside down and inside out? By believing that *they* might be God's men, as well as myself?

Am I willing to entertain the thoughts of others precisely when those thoughts anger me? When they disgust me? Am I willing to believe that such thoughts might be, for me and for my life, a very word from the Lord?

Am I willing to be disturbed by making specific offers of my own self, my time, my energy, my schedules, my talent, my convenience, my experience, my prestige, my business connections, as a personal response and a personal commitment to some human need in the world, preferably a need in whose presence I feel guilty and anxious and fearful and insecure?

Am I willing to be disturbed by the probability that if I do not verify God's aliveness by my own personal commitments in his world, all else I call my "religion" will turn out to be little more than self-deception? Am I willing to be disturbed by living as if that probability were absolute certainty, even though it may be no more than distorted myth?

Am I willing to absorb all threats created by the possibility that what I have called "God" is dead?

To ask such questions and a hundred others like them, and then to let demanding, disturbing answers make their mark upon our lives, is at once the price of renewal and the substance of Christian salvation in our time, secularly, humanly perceived. For struggle with such questions plunges us more deeply into the human, secular scene, the locale of the salvation experience. Such struggle heightens and intensifies that disturbance which is at once the substance and the evidence of salvation.

Small wonder that we hear that disturber of the peace, William Stringfellow, reminding us that salvation is not always sudden or dramatic, but that it is always traumatic.[2] What is beng required of us, writes the Anglican disturber John Robinson in that small bombshell of a book which has helped the church so much because it has upset and disturbed the church so deeply—what is required of us, "reluctant as we may be for the effort involved, is a radically new mould, or *meta-morphosis*, of Christian belief and practice. Such a recasting will, I am convinced, leave the fundamental truth of the Gospel unaffected. But it means that we have to

[2] William Stringfellow, *Free in Obedience* (New York: Seabury Press, 1964), p. 28.

be prepared for *everything* to go into the melting—even our most cherished religious categories and moral absolutes." [3]

That melting process refines for us a second dimension of the liberating insight, a dimension on which we must now focus. It relates to another word in the traditional Christian vocabulary: evangelism. Just as we have turned our understanding of salvation inside out and upside down, so we must turn our understanding and practice of evangelism. We must do with evangelism what we have done with salvation—make it secular, human, and therefore political.

The word politics, has its root in the Greek "polis," city, and "politikos," citizen. Political concerns thus include the whole life of the citizen in the city understood broadly as the complex of forces and realities which form man's environment and shape his life. Thus evangelism is a political category because the man to whom the evangelist would speak effectively about God is not man in a vacuum. The object of evangelistic effort, the one to whom that effort is addressed, is man in a real world, man shaped and formed, blessed and cursed, enobled and degraded, by a whole interacting network of human decisions, judgments, values, and priorities. In that classic Aristotelian sense, Protestant laymen by virtue of their leverage in the decision-making processes of our society are now challenged by God-in-Christ to breathe the breath of his life into Phillipe Maury's assertion that "politics is the language of evangelism." [4]

We must search for the meaning of that strange assertion by dealing at some length with one basic fact on which Christians of all persuasions are agreed: that we cannot effectively speak about the living God, cannot be genuinely evangelical and evangelizing Christians until we find a consensus about that Living God's identity. Who is he? What is he like?

[3] John A. T. Robinson, *Honest to God* (Philadelphia: Westminster Press, 1963), p. 124.

[4] Philippe Maury, *Politics and Evangelism*, trans. Marguerite Wieser (Garden City, N. Y.: Doubleday & Co., 1960), p. 28.

What is his nature? Where is he found? These questions must be asked and answered before we can possibly know what truly evangelical language looks like.

Clearly, if God is an otherworldly, metaphysical being, high and lifted, up, if his nature is best described by words such as omniscience, omnipresence, and omnipotence, then it is immediately obvious that politics in the sense we have just defined it has very little, if anything, to do with God, and that political language could never be the language of evangelism, that is, the language we employ to speak effectively to men about God. To speak of such a God would require a language compounded of philosophy, metaphysics, and religious devotion such as we do, by and large, now employ in the church.

On the other hand, if God is not primarily to be found outside man as the wholly Other making for righteousness, but rather as the One who dwells in man as a divine spark or image or spirit, then it is equally clear that politics could never be the language for effective speaking about God. If God is primarily that kind and quality of inner light, then the language for speaking effectively about him, the language of evangelism, must be primarily the language of the Christian mystics, the language of inner search, self-examination and self-analysis of the kind we usually have in mind when Christians speak of "the inner life." Or to update the matter slightly, bringing it right into our own century through such intellectual giants as Bultmann and Tillich, we should say that if God is that kind of inwardly apprehended Presence or Absence, then the language for speaking about him effectively would be the language of existentialism, the language in which the basic categories of thought are "being and non-being," "existence and nothingness," "despair and anxiety," all these in the context of inner search, search and agony in "the depths."

However, instead of being devotees of the latest fad in theology or philosophy, of jumping like hotheaded young

Turks on the most recently painted bandwagon, instead of unthinkingly accepting traditional answers to the questions of evangelism, that is, instead of creating God after our own image, according to our own desires and predilections—what might happen if we turned away from all the fads in theology and philosophy and sociology to the Bible and asked the question, "What is God like? Where is he found? How is he to be spoken about?"

These are complex questions, but we can give a straightforward answer without oversimplifying their infinite complexity. The answer from the Bible would be this: God is the One who acts in history and whose actions are designed to make men free and responsible. If we were to ask a deeply believing Old Testament Jew, Who is God and what is he like? we would be told of a God who reveals himself by his liberating actions in the lives of men. The Old Testament really knows nothing about God's "qualities" or "attributes" or "essence" in any strictly philosophical or metaphysical way. The Hebrew mind is unphilosophical; it is the genius of the biblical believer to say: "God acts. That is really all I know about him. God is the One who made the universe and me in it. God is the One who delivered me from slavery in Egypt. God is the One who gave me a law at Sinai. God is the One who led me through the wilderness and got me to a new land. When I grew faithless and rebellious and worshiped gods of my own making, he sent me into captivity; there he taught me to sing the Lord's song in a strange land, and when I had learned to sing again, he brought me back home. He did all this to the end and he might send me into all the world to preach good tidings to the poor, to bind up the brokenhearted, to proclaim liberty to the captives, and the opening of prison to them that are bound." The presence, the power, the very life of God-in-Christ are made evident in and through liberating acts, events whose consequence is that men are being set free from various forms of slavery.

If we profess to take the Bible seriously, we must take

seriously the possibility that the living God of the Bible is now where he has always been, namely, wherever men are being helped to assume responsibility for one another and for the whole fabric of common life in which all men share a common destiny. That is what it means to say, "politics is the language of evangelism." It is so because the living God-in-Christ is the God who acts in men's lives in history. If the church now calls all its members to become politically involved, it is precisely because we believe in that Christ, and also because in an urban, technological society such as ours, those involvements are effective ways for us to be witnessing, good-news-bearing, Bible-believing, born-again Christians, in a word, evangelists.

In that profoundly political way, both George and Ken, whom we have been considering above, have been evangelized and have become evangelists, humanly oriented, secular, political evangelists, models for the future. George was evangelized secularly, in the language of politics, by his black and white companions at that interracial confrontation. George's church, in generating that event out of the concern of some of its members for more responsible relationship to racial tensions in Montclair, catalyzed the evangelistic process. Now that the event is over, George is evangelizing politically, that is, humanly and secularly, in his business, in his social life, in his family, in his church, and among his friends in local government, by advocating in countless ways for more responsible personal and institutional commitment to the humanization of those structures which affect the lives of the whole human family in Montclair and in metropolitan Newark.

Ken was evangelized through his attendance at a church where there was uncompromising proclamation of the gospel as liberation—liberation of oppressed people from those slaveries which are the result of human neglect and which can be broken by the assumption of human responsibility for the just ordering of common life. Being so evangelized, Ken made a complex of decisions about his own life which, in turn, has made him a secular, political evangelist, a man who speaks effectively of God by teaching and training young lawyers to make the great corporations of American servants of true justice and bearers of deeper responsibility for the common good. Because his evangelizing is secular and political, Ken speaks effectively of God without naming him. Such is the creative limitlessness of evangelism in the secular era. And such is the second dimension of the liberating insight: evangelism, like salvation, is the diametric opposite of what we have assumed, believed, and practiced.

Harvey Cox affirms and illumines the evangelistic dimensions of the liberating insight when he describes an evangelism that has the feel of our own time and of our own life about it as well as the feel of authority which I believe can come only from the living God.

We speak of God politically whenever we give occasion to our neighbor to become the responsible, adult agent, the full post-town and post-tribal man God expects him to be today. We speak of God whenever we cause him to realize consciously the web of interhuman reciprocity in which he is brought into being and sustained in it as a man. We speak to men of God whenever our words cause him to shed some of the blindness and prejudice of immaturity and to accept a larger and freer role in the fashioning of the instrumentalities of human justice and cultural vision. We do not speak to secular man of God by trying to make him religious, but, on the contrary, by encouraging him to come fully of age, putting away childish things. . . . Speaking about God in a secular fashion requires first of all that we place ourselves at those points where the restoring, reconciling activity of God is occurring. This means that evangelism, the speaking about God, is political . . . and [this further] means that the speaking of God must engage people at particular points, not just "in general." It must be a word about their own lives—their children, their schools, their jobs, their hopes and disappointments. It must be a word to the bewildering crises within which our personal troubles arise—a word which builds peace in a nuclear world, which contributes to justice in an age stalked by hunger, which hastens the day of freedom in a society stifled by segregation. If the word is not a word which

79

arises from a concrete involvement of the speaker then it is not a word of God at all, but empty twaddle.[5]

Such is the depth at which God himself mixes faith and politics. And it is not the prerogative of man, except at the terrible price of rebelling against God by throwing the Bible completely out of the church, to pull asunder what God has joined together. Such is the surging inflow of the tide in a time when the living God is pleading with Protestant laymen to transform those religious ghettos which we now call "churches" into training camps—training camps within which through study, planning, prayer, and worship we shall equip and prepare ourselves for movement into the secular world where God himself is at work in the unfulfilled lives of broken, proud, needy, poor, affluent, educated, ignorant, noble, savage, selfish, despairing, and hopeful men. Such is the shape of our opportunity to speak effectively of God in a world where most people, were the truth known, probably do not believe either that God exists or that he acts. In such a world politics is inescapably the language of evangelism, the knowledge and control of all those experiences and processes through which the individual and corporate lives of the whole human family are fulfilled in freedom, love, justice, and responsibility.

Measurable movement toward such fulfillment will require a new breed of liberated laymen in the Protestant churches. That new breed will experience personal salvation in the context of human secularity that has been described; it will evangelize with a new political language whose alphabet has been spelled out.

But how?

With a new Bible.

It is on that awesome possibility that we must now focus with some fear and trembling, but also with a sense of joy.

[5] Harvey Cox, The Secular City (New York: The Macmillan Company, 1965), pp. 255-56.

Our tools will be historical accuracy, theological sophistication, honesty about our own experience, and a willingness to let God be God on his own terms. These are very sharp tools; no matter how carefully or competently we use them, they are likely to cut deeply, making us wince with the pain of recognition.

VI   The Liberating Dynamic:
A New Bible

In theological language, "canon" is a technical term. It means the collection of writings judged by the Early Church to be the authoritative record of the nature, will, and purpose of God. In brief, canonical books are those the church declared to be God's written Word, the "infallible rule of faith and practice," or what we call "the Bible."

Clearly, if some books were judged by early Christians to be canonical and therefore included in our Bible, there must have been other books that didn't make the grade, books judged less authoritative and therefore uncanonical. Indeed, there were such documents—dozens of them—Gospels, letters, doctrinal statements, and bodies of ethical instruction or "teachings."

These extrabiblical or uncanonical writings were read, studied, in some instances cherished, by the Early Church and accorded places of honor in its life. For the first three centuries of the church's history, there developed a complex process of sifting and sorting, a long period in which the church was gradually making up its mind about what writings had apostolic authorship or authority, and which ones lacked it. Not until the year 367 did there appear a listing of the twenty-seven books we now call the New Testament. At that time Athanasius suggested those twenty-seven books, in contrast to all other candidates, ought to be considered as possessing authority and therefore worthy of being official scriptures for the church. So the church declared the canonical question settled; the boundaries of God's written Word were deemed to have been established; the church, in effect, said to its followers: "You need no longer wonder about what writings are authoritative, for that is now an answered question."

Open your minds to what that means: For at least the first

three hundred years of its life, the church itself was undecided about what was and what was not Holy Scripture! During those vital centuries there was agreement that God could and did reveal himself to man through written words; there was further agreement that some written materials were necessarily more authoritative than others for the believing community. But for at least those three centuries there was no general agreement on a superior or a final list. The problem of the canon remained an open question. There can be no substantial doubt that those early, vigorous, sacrificing, spiritually enlivened and enlivening Christians were much more open-minded, and that they enjoyed much more intellectual freedom about the nature and extent of God's written revelations than we enjoy!

Throughout the medieval period the supposedly answered question kept coming up. The medieval church, without quite realizing it, kept the question open, even as the Roman Church today creates a climate of openness by its insistence that the tradition of the church, along with Scripture, is authoritative for Christian faith and life—as if to say, Yes, God speaks in Scripture, but he also speaks in other things written by man.

When we come to the time of the Reformation, it is essential to remember that the Reformers themselves were also more open-minded than we about the canon. Richard Lyon Morgan is on historically solid ground when he writes,

The Reformers demonstrated an amazing freedom in regard to the canon. Luther had the audacity to claim that four books of the New Testament—Hebrews, James, Jude and Revelation—were not "the proper and certain main books of the New Testament," and to relegate them to a New Testament appendix. In other words, Luther did not want to give these books full canonical status. . . . Reformers such as Karlstadt . . . and . . . Zwingli also raised serious questions about the canon, but later Protestantism did not continue their inquiries.[1]

[1] Richard Lyon Morgan, "Let's Be Honest About the Canon," *The Christian Century*, May 31, 1967, p. 717.

It is one of the tragedies of the Reformation that its free-wheeling, spirit-inspired, creative openness to such questions as the canonical one so soon became rigidity. Dr. Morgan believes, and I think wisely, that this post-Reformation hardening of the arteries in the church happened not so much for theological as for psychological reasons. The need for "a defense mechanism over against the monolithic authority of the church of Rome led the Reformers to stifle further questions . . . and the Bible became a 'paper pope.' . . . During the Reformation freedom to consider the matter emerged briefly, but fear of one authoritarianism (the Roman Catholic Church) led to another (biblicism)." [2]

One example of this post-Reformation rigidity is found in the Constitution of the United Presbyterian Church, U.S.A. I am offering this example because I happen to be Presbyterian and know that ecclesiastical context best. But writing from that limited context does not exclude other Protestants from the implications of my point. The quotation which follows from our Presbyterian Constitution has counterparts in the constituting documents of most major Protestant denominations. The Methodist counterpart, for instance, is found in Article 5, of the Articles of Religion of The United Methodist Church. The part of our Presbyterian Constitution which provides a typical Protestant example is the Westminster Confession of Faith; the other confessional ingredients in that Constitution are the Nicene Creed, the Apostles' Creed, the Scots Confession, the Heidelberg Catechism, the second Helvetic Confession, the Theological Declaration of Barmen, and the Confession of 1967. The first chapter of the Westminster Confession is entitled, "Of the Holy Scripture" and addresses itself directly to the canonical question. After stating that God revealed himself decisively as contained in the books of our present Bible, we find this impossibly paralyzing language: "Those former ways of God's revealing his will unto his people

[2] *Ibid.*, pp. 717-19.

now being ceased. . . ." A few paragraphs later the Westminster Confession says: "The whole council of God is either expressly set down in Scripture or by good and necessary consequence may be deduced from Scripture unto which nothing at any time is to be added whether by new revelations of the Spirit or traditions of men."

What happened is as clear as the nose on Cyrano's face; very human and eminently fallible men did, indeed, substitute "not a book for a church, but a dogma for both." A very human and fallible institution, the church, has for centuries closed its mind and tried to close yours and mine even to the possibility that Almighty God might continue speaking to us, might continue revealing himself to us, might lead us further into knowledge and experience of himself through written documents. In the measure that the church has thus tried to limit God's power to act in our lives and our history, it has demonically and idolatrously played God. Moreover, in the measure that we have permitted the doctrinal statements of the church to limit our understanding and experience of God, we have permitted ourselves to be programmed by the need of all institutional caretakers to protect their own works against the creative and life-renewing leadings of the Spirit.

Therefore to reject—as I do clearly reject—language that boxes God in and whittles God down until we have him neatly reconstructed in our own image, shaped according to our own human historically conditioned specifications (even if that language is found in a typical Protestant document like the Constitution of the Presbyterian Church), is not to undermine the authority of our Bible. Such rejection does not demean the worth of that Bible, nor does it suggest that the present Bible cannot be a valid, decisive vehicle of enlightenment, growth, insight, and truth in and through which God meets man. On the contrary, the rejection of such rigid language is an act of living faith in the God of the Bible. It is an affirmation that the God revealed in Christ is wise enough, powerful enough, free enough, and contemporary enough to go on to the end of time,

85

forever revealing himself in newly emerging written documents.

As a Presbyterian, I am grateful for an action of our General Assembly called, "The Confession of 1967." I am especially thankful for the following alteration of our doctrinal standards found in Section III, Paragraph B, entitled "The Bible."

The Bible is to be interpreted in the light of its witness to God's work of reconciliation in Christ. The words of the Scriptures are the words of men, conditioned by the language, thought forms, and literary fashions of the places and times at which they were written. They reflect views of life, history, and the cosmos which were then current, and the understanding of them requires literary and historical scholarship. The variety of such views found in the Bible shows that God has communicated with men in diverse cultural conditions. This gives the Church confidence that he will continue to speak to men in a changing world and in every form of human culture.

That passage does not address itself directly to the question about reopening the canon. Nonetheless, I want to focus attention on that final sentence: "This gives the Church confidence that he will continue to speak to men in a changing world and in every form of human culture." The implication is clearly that the canon should and indeed must officially be reopened if we are to remain faithful to God in our time. Similar words of Emil Brunner are quoted by Dr. Morgan: "Just as the church of the second, third, and fourth centuries had the right to decide what was 'apostolic,' and what was not, on their own responsibilities as believers, so in the same way every church in every period in the history of the church possesses the same right and the same duty." [3]

That "right" and that "duty" bring us closer to the heart of the reason why the canon must be reopened. The closing of the canon was a historically, culturally, politically, and psychologically conditioned action of men. It was fallible because these men like ourselves were quite capable of mistaken judgments. It was not then and is not now a mark of the church's

[3] *Ibid.*, p. 717.

spirituality to absolutize that which is relative, or to declare ultimate, final, and completed that which of necessity and by nature is neither ultimate nor final nor completed, but proximate, tentative, and eminently unfinished.

Examined from its positive aspect, that insight illumines what Paul Tillich calls "the Protestant principle." The Protestant principle is an assertion about the centrality of freedom, creativity, newness and, above all, openness in the activity of God and man and in their relationship to each other in history. In the context of the question about the canon, Tillich affirmed that principle by writing that "the Canon cannot be fixed in a definite way for the partial openness of the Canon is a safeguard of the spirituality of the church." It recognizes and honors the open-ended quality of truth itself. The canon must be reopened because truth cannot be sealed in, closed off, and made predictable.

Summarily, the canon must be opened because it *is* open, whether the church admits it or not.

This is not to say that the present Bible lacks authority, or fails to reveal God, or is unimportant, or can no longer be a meeting place for God and man. Not at all. But it is a most confident affirmation that the Word of God cannot be and is not contained in, or circumscribed by, or limited to, or made secure within, the walls of the present canon. The Word of God is free, open, emerging, undetermined. It is as unconfined and unconfinable as those gloriously open affirmations at the beginning of Genesis 1. "In the beginning God created the heavens and the earth. The earth was without form and void, and darkness was upon the face of the deep; and the Spirit of God was moving over the face of the waters. And God said, 'Let there be light'; and there was light." The word of God is as unconfined and unconfinable as those equally open affirmations with which the Gospel of John launches us into the depths of truth: "In the beginning was the Word, and the Word was with God, and the Word was God. He was in the beginning with God; all things were made through him, and without him was not anything made that was made."

Small wonder that the writer of the Fourth Gospel, so concerned as he is with assuring his readers that the unconfinable Word of God is as inescapable as flesh, ends his written record with this strangely, powerfully enigmatic statement: "There are also many other things which Jesus did; were every one of them to be written, I suppose that the world itself could not contain the books that would be written." The unconfinable Word is confined in flesh, then unconfined again, let loose in history, where the story of his aliveness cannot be completed but only written over and over in a hundred million, trillion ways.

"The world itself could not contain the books that would be written." What an affirmation with which to conclude the one book which the church has canonized, inwardly, perhaps more than any other! What an insight for such a writer of such a book to end such an effort with such an affirmation of openness to the other books that surely will be ours to read as the unfolding story of Jesus' presence in human history emerges in a canon that has no walls around it. What an invitation to embrace the demanding and exciting discipline of finding out for ourselves where and when and by whom the Holy Scriptures of God are still being written! That God, revealed in Christ, surely is wise enough, powerful enough, free enough, and contemporary enough to go on revealing himself in written documents, to the end of time.

That certainty reminds me of the front and back cover on an American Bible Society translation of the New Testament called, *Good News for Modern Man*. It is a splendidly contemporary translation, but what I really want to illumine is the cover. The front cover of course carries the title, but all the rest of the cover space, front and back, is taken up by line drawings of newsprint on which are superimposed at random the mastheads of newspapers now published in every corner of the earth. So designed, that cover becomes one of the symbols of all times, for it asserts that if we who claim Christ's name want the New Testament to become in our lives a living and renewing Word of God, if we want the New Testament to be experienced as *Good News for Modern Man*, then before we read it, while we read it, after we read it steadily we must concurrently search the history and writings of our own times for the Word of God. With a greater discipline, a deeper passion, a truer insight we must discern the Presence, the Power, and the living Word of God written in the circumstances of our own history. What is in the Holy Book cannot be good news for modern man except in the measure that we search for the Word of God in the history of our own times—*The Manila Times*, the *Japan Times*, *The Times of India*, *The Times of London*, the *East African Standard*, *The Sydney Morning Herald*, *The Atlanta Journal*. There is *no* Word of God for the church or in the church, and the church has no good news for modern man—none—except in the measure that you and I do exactly what the early Christians did: search for the Word of God, confront and be willing to be confronted by the Word of God, not in some abstract, spiritual vacuum of a piety detached from history, but rather in the joyous, cruel, glorious, enigmatic, challenging, deadening, frightening, boring, searing, troubling, enlivening, crippling, sobering, intoxicating maelstrom of our own history. The Bible will become in the church and in our lives what it now patently is not, the living Word of God, when we responsibly accept the problems of our history as the raw material of eternity, and in so doing proclaim freely, openly, joyously that the Holy Bible is still being written.

But by whom? Exactly where is that Scripture? How can we identify it? How can we know? How can any man have certainty that something nonbiblical he has read is a Word from the Lord, or contains or communicates such a Word of God? What is to deliver us from a situation of total chaos in which every Tom, Dick, or Harry can lay his hand on any written thing and claim that it is a Word of God? Years ago I drove daily past a church in West Philadelphia. It had a grotesquely huge sign outside which said, "This is everybody's church, worshiping everybody's Christ." I used to read that sign and think, my god, how awful! What a free-for-all! I realize that the same accusation of anarchy could now be leveled at what I am saying about the canon. So the question remains: What *is* to deliver us from a situation in which any man and everyman would become a self-proclaimed authority, so that the church in the very process of seeking guidance for its life would become a meaningless babble of conflicting voices?

That decisive question reminds us that new canonical criteria must be created. The criteria which served the Early Church and the Reformers will not do for us, for we are not called to be Christ's servants in the first or the sixteenth, but in the twentieth century. The God whose Word we would discern is One who speaks to us in the aliveness of our own history. Because that is the sort of God in whom we live, move, and have being, I have no doubt that the new criteria will emerge, and that they will have a lot to do with our willingness to be disturbed. I have proposed that disturbance must now become a new theological category if we are to experience the content of salvation personally in a secular era. Now I am expanding that suggestion by affirming that such disturbance will also be decisive as a criterion of canonicity. As we search for the Word of God written in our own time, I believe we shall often find it in political, literary, and artistic materials which shake the very foundations of our lives, written material with which we shall often vehemently disagree—so deep is the somnolent complacency of our religious isolation from the bedrock problems of our own time. The best example is racial tension and conflict, to which I shall return momentarily in a discussion of the Kerner Commission Report [4] as the Word of God. Suffice it for now to say that the disturbance which will inform and sustain our search for the Word of God will characteristically bring us to those points in the fabric of our

[4] *Report of the National Advisory Commission on Civil Disorders* (New York: E. P. Dutton, 1968).

common life where the most oppressed of God's children are feeling the sharpest pain.

The new canonical criteria will also have something decisive to say about the sovereignty of Christ. The time has come for the church to put up or shut up with regard to our two-thousand-year-old insistence that he is the Lord of life and history. If Christ is, in fact and truth, the sovereign Lord we have proclaimed him to be, the new criteria of canonicity will teach us to live with the probability that such a Lord, in the midst of a secular era which is his own creation, may, probably will, and assuredly can reveal himself in documents making no mention of his name, but which do spell out in concrete, secular terms the political, economic, cultural, sociological, and psychic implications of his life, teaching, death, and resurrection. They will teach us to look for the Word of a sovereign Lord in legislative documents, in business documents, in scientific, artistic, and government documents and, least of all perhaps, in what we have been pleased for some time to call moral, spiritual, and religious documents. Thus, another new criterion of canonicity might well be labeled anonymity or hiddenness or sovereignty in secrecy. And, as with the criterion of disturbance, the underlying question would be the same both for the individual and for the church: Does this written word involve me (us), inextricably, responsibly, and creatively, in the felt suffering of the least privileged of God's children? Does it call me (us) commandingly to their side and establish me (us) as their fellow sufferer(s) and advocates(s)?

That brings us back to the Report of the Kerner Commission. This Commission was appointed by President Johnson to study and analyze the urban rebellions of 1967 and to make recommendations about the solution of those problems to which the rebellions pointed.

By applying the criteria of canonicity—disturbance and sovereignty in secrecy or anonymity—the Report of the Kerner Commission could and should have been perceived by the Christian churches of America as the very Word of God, a new

91

chapter in the Holy Scriptures. It identified institutionalized white racism as the primal cause of those rebellions. At least that part of the report should have been perceived and responded to as Holy Scripture by the churches. For our massive personal and institutional denial of that basic premise makes it impossible to spell out the secular implications of Christ's birth, teaching, death, and resurrection in the urban ghettos of American society. The Report of the Kerner Commission did not become for us and our society a living, saving Word because we refused to let its principal message from the Lord disturb us into awareness and responsibility.

It did not become a living, saving experience of God in the new Bible because we would not permit its insight about institutionalized white racism to bring healing to our diseased condition, either in the churches or in the society as a whole. Disturbance as a criterion of canonicity relates not only to a document's power to disturb us but also, in a prior sense, to our willingness to be disturbed. Therefore, whether we consider the Report's own intrinsic potential for disturbance or our refusal to be disturbed by it, it becomes on either count a prime candidate for canonization.

As for the other criterion—anonymity or hiddenness or sovereignty in secret—the Kerner Report qualifies beautifully. It does not theologize or moralize. It describes, analyzes, concludes, and recommends, but always in purely sociological, economic, political, i.e., totally secular terms. Its origin was a great national crisis, and its creator a president of the United States seeking ways to hold together a whole nation splitting apart at its most secular seams. The Report meets this criterion because it does indeed affirm those truths, insights, and understandings about ourselves and our society which, in sum, the church identifies as the dynamic ingredients of Christ's Kingdom. It makes this affirmation of his sovereignty anonymously, hiddenly, secularly.

For basically the same reasons, the churches of America should have received the essential message of the Black Manifesto as the Holy Written Word of God. For the Black Manifesto is a scream of pain from children of God who are hurting ultimately. That scream of pain from them is God's voice, and it behooves us to receive the words spoken by that voice as his, especially when the words are written down. Indeed, any document which helps us feel that pain of his children stands in the line of holy history and waits to be recognized by the church as its "infallible rule of faith and practice."

This does not mean that everything written now is the Word of God. But it does mean that when you and I read any play, any novel, any editorial, any news of the day, any interpretation of a riot or a war or an arrest for the pushing of drugs, a government report, or an essay on crime, or a love poem, or a letter from a friend, or the angry grafitti scrawled on a subway wall—we must read with our eyes wide open to canonical possibilities. Or when we read a short story of Tolstoy, or Martin Luther King's *Letter from a Birmingham Jail*, or *Renewal*, or Tom Hayden, or Tom Wicker, or *Peanuts*, or John Gardner, or Nicholas Berdyaev, or Noam Chomsky, or *motive*, or Paul Goodman, or Michael Harrington, or Dag Hammarskjöld, or Edward Albee, or George Bernard Shaw, or Winston Churchill, or an obituary, or an ad that makes us want something we don't need, or a letter that makes us want something in relationship to a loved one which we do need but cannot quite have—we must read with our eyes wide open to canonical possibilities. Or when we read the stock market reports, or an old diary written in the days of youth before we gave up hope, or a school newspaper, or a prayer on a church bulletin, or a shopping list for the A & P, or the casualty reports from Vietnam—when we read anything at all which reflects upon, communicates about, agonizes over a demanding, jarring confrontation with the bedrock realities of our lives and our history, the real problems and needs of our own times, then we must read with our eyes wide open to canonical possibilities.

Such canonical possibilities cannot be explored except as we examine in depth the evidence from our own experience. This

93

will be very difficult terrain. For as soon as we begin that examination we move into the realm of subjectivity where it is easy to be misled and natural for a mass of personal judgments to bog us down in spiritual and psychological anarchy. For that reason, it is at once natural and easy to steer away from this area of concern, as I am tempted to do. But we cannot responsibly evade it; the evidence from our own experience, however subjective, however liable to misinterpretation and distortion, is crucial. Without it and apart from it, all the historical and theological evidence we have been probing collapses into insignificance and reduces what we have been attempting to irresponsible, intellectual gamesmanship or worse.

By evidence from our own experience I am recording what has actually happened in many of our lives, namely, that the Word of God has come to us through the reading of nonbiblical materials. I specify nonbiblical or extrabiblical materials—not unbiblical or antibiblical, but merely nonbiblical materials, that is, written materials other than the Bible. Most of us have had experiences of life-giving, life-renewing reorientation through such reading. Perhaps some of us have been more conscious than others of the dimensions involved in such experience, for some of us may well be more open than others to the possibility that God is One who speaks when, where, and how it pleases him to speak, One who cannot be and is not confined within the barriers built by men, even when men decorate those barriers with the tapestries of sanctity, piety, and holy doctrine.

As we search for the Word of God written in our time and verified in our own lives, I believe we shall sustain the search through a vastly deepened experience of the work and power of the Holy Spirit. On the eve of his crucifixion Jesus made some amazing statements to his disciples about the Holy Spirit and the future. They are summed up in the affirmation in John 16:13, where Jesus looks out across the coming eons of time and says: "The Spirit of truth . . . will guide you into all the truth." He made that promise not just to those twelve

94

disciples but also, somehow as in a mystery, to all men in all time. And that group includes us.

More than thirty years ago Sir Edwyn Clement Hoskyns, a New Testament scholar in Corpus Christi College, Cambridge, died. For at least fifteen years before his death he had been working on a historical and theological analysis of the Gospel of John, and it was still unfinished at his death. First published in 1940 under the editorship of Frances Noel Davey, Hoskyns' work of a lifetime, called *The Fourth Gospel*, remains a definitive theological treatise on John's Gospel. Commenting on the passage in John 16:13, Hoskyns wrote these enigmatic sentences:

He shall guide you into all truth, that is, not into further new truth, but into the whole truth concerning that which was concretely and concisely set forth by the Son of God. . . . His [the Spirit's] action does not consist in delivering new truths to the disciples, but in providing a larger, deeper, and more perfect understanding of the teaching which Jesus had given them.[5]

It is precisely that "larger, deeper, and more perfect understanding" of the gospel into which we are now being led by the Spirit. The Spirit, at work in us as the Lord and giver of Life, is creating that understanding with the result that the lid on the canon is loose and coming off. To believe in the Holy Spirit as the creator of that movement is to affirm the breakdown of barriers, the flow of life, the collapse of frameworks and systems and world views and rigidities of doctrine. To affirm that Spirit is to let God be God and, in consequence, to know in our depths that the story of Christ's aliveness in history can never be fully told. To believe in that Holy Spirit is to sense that the gospel must be told and will be told in ways that are ever new, ever emerging, unheard of, unknown, undreamed of, boundless and endless in form and content and structure, unconfined and unconfinable.

[5] Edwyn Clement Hoskyns, *The Fourth Gospel*, ed. Francis Noel Davey (London: Faber and Faber, 2nd ed., 1947), p. 486.

To believe in that Holy Spirit is to affirm a Christ so sovereign that he reveals himself in eternally unfathomable newness, speaking when, where, and as he chooses, using not only those instruments of communication which the church has blessed, but any instruments of communication whatsoever that enable him to get said with power what he wants said when, where, and as it pleases him to say it. Such is the sovereignty of a Holy Spirit who will not be hemmed in by what men choose to call religious, or limited within those boundaries men try in vain to build around God's Word. Such is the sovereignty of One who will not be confined to those expressions men find acceptable. The Spirit-sovereignty has always kept the canon open, whether the church has admitted its openness or not. The Spirit-sovereignty fills us with fear and trembling as it creates the felt possibility that there is no escape from God. But it is that same Spirit-sovereignty which fills us with hope, confidence, and even joy. For it suggests, ineluctably, that God-in-Christ may turn out to be what we have professed but never really believed him to be, namely, the living source of all human possibility.

To comprehend all these weighty matters or even to begin comprehending them is manifestly a big order, terribly hard to fill and frightening. So to open our eyes is a terrifying responsibility, an incredibly heavy burden—as when boys grow up and become men. Little tasks are for little people; trite jobs are for trite men; childish responsibilities are for children. When we are children our speaking, feeling, acting, reading, and thinking are adequately and appropriately those of a child. But when a child matures and becomes a man, what then? Man come of age assumes responsibility by leaving behind the evidences of his immaturity. Among the children's games he no longer plays, indeed, refuses to play, are those called "Let's Play God," and "Let's Box God In." Man grown up, mature, come of age, lives with a demanding, exciting, troubling, intuitive awareness that God speaks as he will, and an equally pervasive awareness that perceiving the Word of God is, therefore, an ever unfolding process, taxing all human capacity for perception, now and to the end of time.

What is specifically involved in that coming of age? What are the raw materials of our maturity? How can we understand ourselves as those moving from childhood and adolescence into genuine spiritual adulthood? In what sense is that adulthood our destiny? What depths of pain are felt by those who finally grow up? What joy do they know? What is the liberating experience?

These are the questions we must now confront—not like those who gamble casually, but rather like those who play for keeps.

VII The Liberating Experience: Adulthood

When a boy is ten or twelve, he is still an essentially dependent creature. He must lean on parents, teachers, an educational system, on friends, family, and peer groups. But as he moves along through those years when he is first sixteen, then eighteen, then twenty, gradually that boy becomes a man. He matures: sexually, emotionally, socially. In brief, he "comes of age." In the measure of his maturity he ceases to be a dependent creature and becomes independent. He moves toward freedom.

We recognize this maturity as a good thing. We do all we can to help our sons achieve it and are unhappy in the measure they fail to achieve it, for we know they are meant for manhood, not boyhood; meant for maturity, freedom, independence, and responsibility, not for childish, restricting dependence. Mature parents want their sons to come of age; we fathers particularly do whatever we can to nourish and sustain the whole complex of experiences within which our sons grow up.

Revolutionaries especially in the church are begining to grasp that man himself, man generically, from the beginning of time has been engaged in that same process of maturation. One phrase now being attached to that long historical development is "the coming of the secular era." To speak of the coming of the secular era is to describe historically the whole mass of political, scientific, sociological, and psychic forces in and through which man has moved and is moving toward maturity.

One consequence of man's coming of age is that he feels less need for his favorite adolescent prop: religion. "Religion" here is used as a technical term with precise content and meaning. We shall come to that substance presently, but first I want to

98

underline one fact: To identify "religion" as an adolescent crutch for little boys is not the same thing as doing away with God, or Jesus Christ, or the Bible. But it is an insistence that God, Christ, and the Bible, preeminently including the Bible as it is still being written, are understood and experienced by little boys and grown men in fundamentally different ways. "When I was a child,"—this is Paul's way of spotlighting the difference—"I spoke like a child, I thought like a child, I reasoned like a child; when I became a man, I gave up childish ways."

During infancy, childhood, and adolescence you have needs which others can fulfill, problems others can help you solve or at least face. But in adulthood you set about facing and working out your own problems. This does not mean that modern, secular man is irrepressibly arrogant or falsely proud. It certainly does not mean that he fulfills his life in isolation from other people. It means that man has come to a point in his long historical development where he no longer needs and will reject, at first subconsciously, then gradually with conscious power and purpose, those childhood and adolescent dependency relationships which do basic violence to the ongoing processes of his own maturity. Just as a son at first subconsciously, then with conscious purpose, rejects whatever there is in his dependency relationships to his father that does violence to the ongoing processes of his maturity, so does man generically.

This does not mean that a son who comes of age ceases to be related to his father. But it does signify a radically reoriented father-son relationship. Moreover, to the degree that their maturity is genuine, they both rejoice that the reorientation is radical. Radical-ness is what validates their love for each other.

As we all know, modern man is not very religious. One fine young man in his late thirties, just before being ordained as an Elder, told me how uncomfortable he felt because, as he put it, "I'm not a very religious guy." Over the years I have heard scores of fine men make the same self-estimate. "I'm not very religious." Always apologetically. Such is modern, secular man's understanding of himself. It is an accurate self-perception. He is not very religious. But instead of crying about it, let us rejoice: it is because he is growing up. It is because man is built in such a way that he will reject whatever does violence to his own basic, God-given nature.

We must be specific about what it is that man come of age rejects because he no longer needs it and because its use demeans him. Eberhard Bethge, interpreter and close friend of Dietrich Bonhoeffer, identifies four conceptual areas in which man come of age is throwing a lot of baggage overboard. These four complexes of thought, feeling, doctrine, institution, and history bound together are what I have previously called the technical content and meaning of religion. They are

(1) all forms of religious individualism in the measure that they keep man from penetrating the "mystery of communal life";

(2) all metaphysics, all supernaturalisms (beyond the physical or material) which locate reality outside man's known world and thereby provide an escape from that world;

(3) all compartmentalized concepts which make Christianity "one part of life," that is, something identified in separateness or isolation from life in its totality;

(4) all concepts of God which make God a machine for providing answers, solving problems, dispensing solutions, help, comfort, etc.[1]

Many creative thinkers in the church are now asking us to understand and believe that for modern man, man come of age and set free, that is, for scores of thousands of laymen and laywomen, Christianity must be religionless in the sense that it must have extracted from it at least those four time-honored elements. These primal ingredients of the tradition must be

[1] See Eberhard Bethge, in *Chicago Theological Seminary Register*, February 1961; quoted in C. W. Williams, *Faith in a Secular Age* (New York: Harper & Row, 1966), pp. 60-61.

isolated, diagnosed as death-dealing, and surgically removed from our understanding of Christianity because men come of age, that is, the strongest laymen of our Protestant churches, are crippled by them. These ingredients of religion which once served us well are now integral to our spiritual retardation, and our effort to throw them off is the best evidence available for the existence in us of something elemental making for health and wholeness. We no longer need these ingredients in order to survive with a growing sense of meaning, dignity, and purpose in our lives. Moreover, we are now beginning to understand that those four time-honored elements never were integral to the essence of Christian faith and life but only tacked on to it because man needed them while he was still in his infancy, childhood, and adolescence.

But what is left? If we remove all that, is anything left at all? In pain, frustration, and anger many will cry out, "Are you trying to take everything away?" I would respond to that disturbing, terrifying question by saying, as Jesus did shortly before his death, "Hear another parable. There was a householder who planted a vineyard, and set a hedge around it, and dug a wine press in it, and built a tower, and let it out to tenants, and went into another country." (Matthew 21:33.) Consider the possibility that the decisive fact in that parable is this: After the owner of the vineyard departed, all that remained was the vineyard itself and the tenants and the chance that they might be responsible in it, to themselves, to and for one another, to the owner in his absence. That is a lot. It is enough for man come of age.

What remains after God in his wisdom departs from us and leaves us alone, what remains after history takes away from us those understandings of God appropriate for infants and children and adolescents, is not just the strain and tension and fighting and killing among the tenants, but also the possibility of responsible adulthood. What we have left after the death of certain concepts, after the demise of religion, after God goes away and leaves us, is the whole vineyard, that

101

is, the world, ourselves and one another, and the possibility of using all that as the raw material of maturity. In one of his letters from prison (July 16, 1944), Bonhoeffer comes exactly to the point:

The only way to be honest is to recognize that we have to live in the world *etsi deus non daretur* [as if God did not exist]. And this is just what we do see—before God! So our coming of age forces us to a true recognition of our situation *vis à vis* God. God is teaching us that we must live as men who can get along very well without him. The God who is with us is the God who forsakes us (Mark 15:34). The God who makes us live in this world without using him as a working hypothesis is the God before whom we are ever standing. Before God and with him we live without God.[2]

"The world of the parables," writes Albert Van den Heuvel, commenting on that story of the absent owner in Matthew 21,

is "a world without God" in which the test given to man is precisely that of living *etsi Deus non daretur*—as if God did not exist. We should understand that phrase rightly. It does not say we should live as we do *quia Deus non daretur*—because God does not exist—but it says that just because he is this God who goes abroad and leaves the vineyard to his servants, he requires this life of faith which is lived as seeing the invisible by those who have not seen and still believe. That means living like the Messiah who renounced all claims on heavenly troops.[3]

To renounce, as that disturber of our peace did, all claim on heavenly troops, to slough off "religion" as it has been defined, to be a secular man, and to come of age are merely different ways of describing what is, in fact, happening in our own time and in our own lives. Such words and phrases are creeping into the language of the church in recognition of a movement which is broadly historical, engulfing all cultures.

[2] *Letters and Papers from Prison*, p. 219 (Paperbacks Ed.).
[3] A. H. Van den Heuvel, *The Humiliation of the Church* (Philadelphia: Westminster Press, 1966), pp. 42-43.

But it is also profoundly individual and personal, touching all our lives, telling it "like it is" about what we are experiencing. It is a movement from slavery to freedom, from unconsciousness to awareness, from phoniness to authenticity, from shallowness to depth, from adolescence to adulthood, from religion to Christ. As that progression occurs within us and among us, we recognize that men have always

attempted to conceal the nakedness of faith, although, of course, theologians have always talked about it, with laws, systems, cathedrals, and ministries; and it seems that only in our century is it all put to the test. What God could not do through the right hand of his church, he had to do through the left hand of science, atheism, the analysis of language, and the people's loss of the organ of religion. We realize now that God went abroad and left the vineyard to us—and it is to us in the plural. It is good to remind ourselves that we have nothing left but each other, and that therefore the thing we have to work out from there is the mystery of communal life.[4]

As we penetrate that mystery we shall be privileged to understand the end of the parable in Matthew 21. It is true that the owner of the vineyard went away and that he never returned. When all hell broke loose in the vineyard, the owner sent servants to repair the damage. That didn't work because they were killed, so he sent his son, and the son was killed. So it is that after "the death of God," after that death of that God, there is indeed something left for those men come of age who claim the name of Christ, something in addition to and consequent upon his assumption of responsibility, namely, the possibility in us of a creatively "cruciform response."

Set free from all the excess religious baggage he collected during his infancy, childhood, and adolescence, Christian man come of age is free at last to live by dying, that is, to be "in Christ" by being totally for others, especially those others who are still in some form of bondage. Unencumbered by religion, mature man is free to be present in the nonreligious,

[4] *Ibid.*, p. 45.

unreligious, irreligious, sacrilegious world as Jesus was present in it—present in weakness, in powerlessness, through identity with and responsible relationship to the needs of other men because, where, and as they suffer. Man come of age is free to stop being religious and to become Christian by becoming *human*.

"To be a Christian," wrote Bonhoeffer from his prison cell shortly before his death, "does not mean to be religious in a particular way, to cultivate some particular form of asceticism (as a sinner, a penitent, a saint) but to be a man. It is not some religious act which makes a Christian what he is, but participation in the suffering of God in the life of the world." [5] Such is the shape of that creatively cruciform response which will increasingly identify those mature men come of age to whom the future belongs because they accept responsibility for it. That response is the informing dynamic of the revolution.

When the Bible insists that Creation, Fall, and Redemption are inseparable motifs in one story of salvation, it does so by binding them together with the common thread of man's responsibility for the creation. Just as sin and evil are to be understood as man's turning away from his role as a responsible cocreator with God, so are repentence, salvation, and redemption to be understood as man's turning back to the resumption of that responsibility. In sum, that responsibility is man's for man. Harvey Cox, more than others, has helped us understand that it is responsibility for bringing order and purpose out of the formless, chaotic void of man's relationships to the creatures and the creation. "As you have done it to the least of these my brothers," said Jesus in ageless, cosmic commentary on the creation accounts of early Genesis, "you have done it to me." It is Jesus as Lord of our lives who urges us to yield to the humanist impulse, for it is in yielding to it that his sovereign lordship is confessed and affirmed as very truth of very truth.

[5] *Letters and Papers from Prison*, pp. 222-23 (Paperbacks Ed).

So we come to a new, life-giving insight into what faith is, what it really means to depend on the biblical God and to trust that God. So do we grow into a new awareness of what it takes to lean on the everlasting arms of the Lord. We depend on God in the measure that we act as those who believe about ourselves what the Bible tells us: that we are the responsible finishers of a creative process begun by God and turned over to us. When we move away from that responsibility for one another into any disobedience to the humanist impulse, we suffer the felt evil of alienation from our brothers because that disobedience is denial of the lordship of Christ. His lordship is affirmed only as our obedience to that impulse is full and free.

If man is not doing such a great job of obeying that impulse fully and freely, not really being a first-rate cocreator of the universe, if he is not bringing order out of chaos, not coming of age as rapidly as the needs of the time demand, then the church must assume major responsibility for that failure. For the church has taught us all an understanding of dependence on God which is at once unbiblical and sub-Christian. That distortion is part of our mental furniture, it cripples us, it keeps us from depending on God by depending on ourselves as the self is biblically constituted. That distortion obscures the fact that "faith" is not Emersonian self-reliance or some new form of human arrogance, for it is rooted in solid biblical anthropology.

This is not meant to be so theoretical, heady, and conceptual that some reader might get the notion I am not writing about real people. Therefore I want to return to Bill whom I have described before. I said that John is the nearly perfect product of a corrupt system, and that Bill is the product of that system's collapse. To be more specific I would like to affirm that the systemic collapse perceived by Bill is precisely the collapse of what I am here identifying as "religion." Bill is what he is and where he is, in Central Church, exactly because he has

105

stopped being "religious" and is therefore becoming Christian. He is a man come of age, a new creation.

His maturity creates for Bill the agonizing question about his relationship to the church: Can he remain faithful to Christ and stay in it? Bill is drifting away from the church, not because he has lost his faith in the lordship of Christ, but because he has found that faith. Because Central Church, all its openness and creativity notwithstanding, is still living in the style and era of Christian religion rather than Christian faith and life, Bill is essentially tolerated rather than valued in Central Church. His very maturity and integrity are what militate principally against his being recognized as a strong light at the end of a long, dark tunnel. Not that Bill's attitude toward the church is primarily informed by an adolescent need to be appreciated in Central Church. His aching thirst for the water of Life in a desert of Christian religion is tempting him to discern the Body of Christ through non-religious commitments to the relief of human pain. A typical instance of such commitment would be his deep involvement in the New Community Corporation, which is trying to spark the emergence of a fuller humanity in Newark's Central Ward, the area of Newark where the rebellions of 1967 were most destructively waged. Bill's personal knowledge of the Lord Jesus through his secular commitments to the restoration of the human community and his use of politics as the language of Christian evangelism have sustained and nourished in him a creatively religionless maturity. That very maturity makes him so unacceptable to John. Bill is a profound threat to John, a salvational disturbance in John's depths, because Bill is a living reminder to John of the fact that God—the God of the written and still being written Bible revealed secularly in Jesus Christ— cannot and for the most part does not go to church any more. It is too damned religious.

Bill understands that John F. Kennedy set the theological tone for our era by reminding us that what our Judeo-Christian heritage finally comes to is an inner assurance that the works of

God can only be our own. Having come of age, Bill understands that any doctrine, liturgy, institution, any piety, any understanding of prayer or worship or ethics, any formulation of spirituality which conceals, compromises, or waters down that essential truth does violence not only to the written and still being written Bible, but also to our own deepest experiences of life. Any denial of that truth negates God, demeans man, and denigrates Christ by trying to keep us in our spiritual childhood and adolescence.

There is still at work in our society a powerful conspiracy of religious concepts, ideas, value systems, and power structures, all of which must be resisted and overcome. A long struggle lies ahead of us, especially in the church. But in the end that conspiracy shall not prevail. It must not prevail, indeed, it cannot prevail, for

now in the fullness of time, man has discovered the deep secret of history . . . , he has risen to a new perception. Nothing in the universe exists except the onrushing givenness of chaos. It is only human rationality that creates patterns and imposes order on all that is. . . . Man places an overlay of order on reality and creates the universe. . . . Experiencing himself as an agent in the creation of the future, Man has felt the claim of the inescapable task to predict the future and so to create it. There are no immutable laws relentlessly grinding out his destiny. Rather, there are powers and forces and probabilities, all of which he relates to as the controller and determiner. Man come-of-age is the master of his own destiny. . . . This is both his gift and his burden. He is no longer privileged to escape into the stance of victim. He is required to take charge. No longer can history be regarded as an inevitable happening. No longer can we point to one aspect of life, the economic, the political, as the source of power and patterns which create the future. No longer can we wait, confident that tomorrow will produce acceptable alternatives to the present. The universe is dependent on us. It is our responsibility. . . . It is a matter of freedom; the freedom to affirm our lives, the freedom to possess the universe; and the freedom to create tomorrow. . . . It is a critical turning point in the very destiny of life, itself. No longer are we merely in search of new laws of nature. We determine the future of the evolutionary drama. We are now deciding the shape of this

107

planet and of self-consciousness, itself. It is not enough to spend one's life in seeking. Each man, alone, and all men, together can and must create. Man is responsible.[*]

God is praised and Jesus Christ as Lord is glorified as we come to understand and believe that obedience to such insight is the cost of our discipleship. What is happeneing throughout the church today is that a steadily increasing, valiant band of grown-up men and women are discovering their urge to meet that cost, to pay that price, to embrace the discipline of that obedience. Their growing commitment is generating fantastic revolutionary pressures inside the warm, cozy womb of the religious system. As that pressure mounts and the system responds by collapsing, an incredibly beautiful complex of new possibilities emerges. Those possibilities are the substance of hope, even as they are the raw materials of revolution in the church.

We must try now to touch and handle them.

[*] "The Declaration of the Spirit Movement of the People of God Century Twenty"; *Image*, Journal of the Ecumenical Institute, No. 5, October 31, 1967, pp. 3-16.

VIII   The Raw Materials of Revolution

The revolution in the church will be sustained and nourished by at least two dynamic forces: (a) the movement of clergy into secular occupations, and (b) an up-ending of theological education. This is not to suggest that other forces will not also be at work, but only that these two must be deeply perceived now, before God-in-Christ abandons the present institutional church.

Advocating revolution in theological education makes it inevitable that many defense mechanisms will be activated, especially in the theological establishment. For such advocacy clearly implies that there is something radically wrong with theological education as we now have it. And this is it: Our seminaries are training the wrong people. Everything this field manual has affirmed about de-professionalizing the ministry is empty talk until the whole church asserts that the principal function of a theological seminary is to train laymen for mission and ministry in the world.

Because God-in-Christ doesn't go to church anymore, is "in the world" and "for the world," and because laymen are, in consequence, the best ministers the church has, we must change our understanding of a theological seminary's very purpose. The nature of ministry calls for revolution at the core. In a church obedient to its own best insights about who ministers are, the work of a theological seminary might peripherally include the training of a few clergy, but their training can no longer be the seminary's rationale. The main purpose of the theological seminaries must now be to create, nourish, and sustain an impulse to mission and to witness in laymen.

This can be done by having laymen train laymen to discern the presence, the activity, and the power of God moving in and through the needs, the pains, the opportunities, the infinitely wondrous complexities of the secular world. The result of such discernments will be a grasping and a being grasped by the powerful content of another great concept which has geen too much talked of and too little lived in recent years: servanthood. In a church enlivened by this revolution in theological education, laymen can and shall be trained for servanthood, vulnerable, sophisticated, insightful servanthood in and for the world.

Many will immediately and responsibly ask, "How could this be so? How could laymen ever have time, to say nothing of motivation, to attend theological seminary? After all, laymen have jobs. They have families. They have other things to do. Why not speak of something that has in it at least the possibility of realization?"

In a technologically oriented society such as ours now is, and a cybernated society such as ours is fast becoming, wherein the three- or four-day-work week is much closer to being "just around the corner" than most of us realize, a decisive question for vast segments of the society will center around the use of "leisure time." For millions of people now working a forty-hour week, leisure time will increase dramatically.

In such a framework it will be no great strain and might well be a blessed deliverance from boredom for enlivened laymen to give two days a week, or parts of those days, preparing themselves for creative engagement with the world God calls the church to serve. In those hours they could embrace the disciplines of study, reading, discussion, and action-training in seminaries become centers for ministry.

What I am proposing, not as a quixotic dream but rather as a practical, possible means of achieving the open ministry, is not only a reformed, but also an expanded system of theological education. In America the magnitude of that expansion might well be to a point where each existing seminary would grow to a hundred times its present enrollment, and the number of completely new centers for ministry would also be very large.

If some protest that such a concept is impossibly unrealistic, I can only say, "not so." Both student body and the faculty for such centers already exist. All that is missing is money, facilities, and motivation. As for money and the things it provides, they are important, demanding considerations, but always secondary in the sense that money is far easier to come by than men's hearts.

More nearly germane is the matter of motivation. In that realm there are no objective proofs, no measureable data. It is one man's subjective judgment against another's. I make no claim to finality or authority for what I am about to write. The case I make for my personal convictional approach rests on the fact that I have, for twenty years in the ministry, listened to laymen. As a result, here is the shape of my manifestly prejudicial position. The clericalism which plagues the professional ministry conceals from us clergy a profound disillusionment laymen feel about the church in general, and ministers in particular. Laymen themselves are only vaguely aware of their disillusionment's extent, and not often are they articulate about it. Because most laymen are not given to acts of intrinsic cruelty, they almost never tell ministers what they really think, feel, and believe about the church and ministers. Laymen are too kind for that, too thoughtful, too mature, too responsible. Laymen tell us clergy many things, but they do not often tell us what they honestly sense about the church, namely, that it is a very human institution, run by a caste of professionals whose incomes, personal securities, careers, and ego structures are bound up with the preservation of most, if not all, presently prevailing institutional priorities. Countless laymen, indeed, perhaps a majority of the most responsible ones, feel this way but never tell us ministers out of considerate concern for us. They also fail to tell it like is because of the guilt we have conditioned them to feel whenever they try to level with us and begin to talk with us as honestly as they talk among themselves in the quiet of their own best meditations. One result is that ministers, for the most part, have not

111

the foggiest notion of what really goes on in lay minds about the clergy and the church.

A single aspect of this blindness—there are many others, but for the moment I confine myself to making certain observations about one—is that clergy consistently sell laymen short, underrate them, demean them. Specifically in the context of our present discussion of theological education, clergy demean and diminish laymen by failing or refusing to grasp the depth of longing for a better way that now prevails in innumerable lay minds. Whenever clergymen discuss the need for stronger, better laymen in the church, the most commonly heard comments are: "But they aren't interested," or, "They're too busy," or, "They simply do not care enough about the gospel," or, "They're too ignorant," or, "What do they know about it?" or, "They're hopelessly rigid."

Such is the dim view most clergy take of most laymen, all our pious mouthings to the contrary notwithstanding. The view is not only dim but also tragic. For it conceals from us the depth of desire for a revolutionized church that now exists in many lay minds. Moreover, it numbs our muscles, so that we clergy can no longer touch and handle the raw materials of a responsible revolution in the church. Those raw materials are: (a) the disillusionment of many laymen with things as they now are in the church; (b) the readiness of large numbers of laymen to move across the threshold of consent into new, undiscovered, undeveloped territory; (c) the daily presence of laymen where God is, that is, in the world. The central theological task is for them to help one another discern that Presence, and then free those laymen to teach a de-professionalized church to practice that Presence secularly, in the renewal and restoration of the human community.

We are failing to nourish the desire for sustained, disciplined thought and research which many laymen are expressing when we clergy stop pontificating long enough to let them speak. That desire is real and seeks expression. It is one of the principal raw materials out of which the necessary commit-

112

ments of time and energy could be fashioned. It constitutes adequate motivational energy for their meaningful participation in the revolution of which I speak. All these considerations undergird the seemingly irresponsible statement that the student body already exists.

But what of the faculty? Who would teach in lay-oriented and lay-dominated seminary student bodies? How would that teaching be informed and sustained? What would be its essential spirit? What would be the nature of leadership in the seminaries become centers for ministry?

In the early stages of the revolution, faculty leadership would necessarily come from both clergy and laymen, with clergy in a rapidly decreasing, secondary and supporting faculty role. Faculty would be those men and women with (a) the best minds, (b) the most comprehensive educations, and (c) the most sustained records of creative, responsible involvement in the secular world because it is God's world and the locale of his saving work. Intellectual leadership resting on those foundations already exists. We have it right now in a few clergy but in far greater quality and quantity in dedicated, committed Christian laymen. Not many clergy or laymen are now acutely aware of this exciting, power-laden resource, because our professionalism blinds both groups to its presence in the church and in the world. We have heard endlessly and still hear a lot of high-sounding obeisant talk about leading laymen. But not for a moment do we clergy really believe them capable of profound, searching, creative, intellectual leadership in and for the church. For the church is now hung up on the false notion that truly intellectual leadership must come from those professionals who are in the academic and spiritual enclaves of theological education. There is only one way adequately to describe that idea: lies! lies! lies! What we have until now understood as the primarily academic life can no longer be the source of intellectual leadership for the church of Jesus Christ, not if we mean what we say about God's being in the world and for the world. Rather, we must

113

understand that intellectual leadership in the church is produced by a marriage of secular discipline and worldly involvement, a union of sophistication about the world and commitment to its humanization in Christ.

This implies much more than obvious changes such as those which bring clergy and laymen together in all study situations. At deeper levels of awareness, it means that every study experience will give to all participants—teachers, clergy, laity—a working base of shared perspective, of common insight, and of mutual concern about the world where God calls them to lose their lives. As the church comes of age and gives deep, inward consent to its own incarnational insights, every period of reflection will of necessity and desire be informed by understanding of those secular realities in the world to which the reflection points. As the church finds courage to fish or cut bait about God's presence in and his passion for the world, it will insist that all theological education shall be an existentially integral part of personal Christian commitment to the church's Lord, validated by personal, vocational presence-in-risk at the scenes of God's action in the secular order, his own creation. That insistence will create and sustain a conceptual and methodological revolution in theological education so profound that the church will never be the same again, unable, hopefully, even to recognize itself in the mirrors of history.

The best news is that this revolution is already happening. In the last twelve months New York Theological Seminary in Manhattan implemented programmatically a conviction that it is just as important to educate laymen as it is to educate clergy. New York Theological Seminary now provides a crucially important model for the future of theological education. Its formal articulation of revolutionary principle comes out like this in the 1970-71 catalog:

The seminary is as much concerned to serve laity as seminarians and clergy. This statement looks tame enough but it is revolutionary: till now, seminaries' efforts at training the laity have been

114

either nonexistent or peripheral. Now this concern has equal status with the original seminary concern, namely, "seminarians" [i.e., post-college students studying for professional religious work], and with a rising concern of these past few years, namely continuing education for clergy [in this catalog, "clergy"].

Since World War II, the Christian world has experienced a lay renaissance, calls for "the renewal of the laity," and rising power of the lay voice in the churches. But adult Christian education has lagged far behind the lay movement. The pathetic result: laity with more power in the churches but without the greater knowledge and the specific skills to use that power to full effect . . . laity with no more power to witness and serve in the world, for such power needs the increased knowledge and specific skills that only lay theological education can provide.

In line with our primary goal of enabling Christians to "do theology," i.e., to acquire the knowledge and skills of the Christian way of seeing and responding, thus refining and implementing one's Christian commitment, our Lay Theological Education programs work from the layman's concrete world to the theological disciplines: the beginning point is where the layman is, not what "the subject" is. To put it another way, "the subject" is the layman himself, the questions he is living and wants help on refining into answers that are better questions. "The scene" is not primarily the classroom, but where the layman is living (his domestic, work, civic, and leisure world); and "the problems" are not those growing out of the academic theological disciplines, but the frustrations the layman is currently experiencing in his efforts to live life humanly and Christianly.

When a seminary takes giant steps like that, committing itself wholeheartedly to the theological education of laymen, what does its curriculum look like? In the case of New York Theological Seminary the courses offered to laymen in the Fall-Winter term for 1970-71 include the following titles, each of which, in a different way, affirms and celebrates the presence of God in the secular order: "The Image Media: Silver Screen and Gold Cross"; "The Urban Scene: The East Village"; "Justice in Public Education"; "Quality of Life: The Environment"; "Woman Power"; "Non-Violence: Pathfinders and the Path"; "Celebrate Life! An Exercise in Global Vision"; "Morality and Modern Political Revolutions"; "Counseling for Lay Workers"; "Education as Rebirth." Such is the wave of the future in theological educational curricula. That future is God's, and as the wave becomes tidal, sweeping away most current theological education, one can hope that an institution like New York Theological Seminary will fulfill its promise by becoming progressively less concerned about the education of professional clergy, while concurrently strengthening its excitingly future-oriented concern for the theological education of laymen.

Another hopeful dynamic in "the greening of theological education" in America is the action training movement. Since 1964 when the Urban Training Center opened in Chicago, more than twenty such centers have come into being around the country. While these Action-Training Centers are not in any way related to theological seminaries and operate independently of them, they nevertheless constitute and offer decisive models for the future of theological education. They are lay-oriented and their main priority is liberation "for blacks, browns, reds, poor whites, alienated youth, women and disaffected decision makers within social institutions." [1]

The action training movement is one to which the theological education establishment must pay closest attention and from which it must take many cues, precisely because it is a method for "doing theology," and "sees itself as subsidiary to mission and the place of that mission among the most oppressed and poorest of the city. Action training calls for a direct engagement in social problems and the development of skills to deal with them. . . . It is a process of teaching and learning how to effect institutional change through supervised experiences of engagement in social problems and reflection upon that engagement." [2]

[1] *JSAC Grapevine:* Vol. 2, No. 4, October 1970, Joint Strategy and Action Committee, New York.
[2] *Ibid.*

I hope that seminary faculties and administrators across America will take these Action-Training Centers as "a word from the Lord" and learn to "do theology" with them. Shining, substantial hope inheres in the possibility that existing seminaries, Action-Training Centers, denominational structures like Presbyterian Presbyteries, Methodist Conferences, Episcopal Dioceses, and most importantly local congregations will form new theological education coalitions in which issue-oriented secularly grounded training for laymen will provide a de-professionalized ministry for the church of the future.

That desperately needed and finally irrepressible educational phase of the revolution will be nourished and sustained by a concurrent movement upon whose dynamic we must now try to touch. I predict that in this present century we shall see a steadily growing movement of ordained clergy from their present church jobs into secular employment. Let me move still further toward the end of the limb by affirming that the church should welcome this movement, identify it as a work of the Holy Spirit, and, so believing, seek to be creatively and responsibly related to this movement.

Immediately, I am quite aware, some will try to saw off that limb and in anticipation exult in the resulting crash by asking, "What proof do you have? What facts do you have to support your case? Where is your evidence?" These are entirely fair questions, and I look upon any man who asks them as one engaged in a reasonable act. Therefore, by way of immediate response I admit that in any common sense of their normal usage I have neither facts, evidence, nor proof. I repeat, in the normal sense of their usage. For I simply do not believe that questions raised at such deep levels are ever answered by "facts" in any normative sense. Nor do I believe that a man's duty to think at those levels is either compromised or diminished by the unavailability of such empirical proof for his central affirmations.

Everything, or nearly everything, I long to share in this regard is objectively indemonstrable. The main authority these

117

opinions possess inheres in honest concern for the church's health and genuine desire for her welfare. I recognize this is close to saying that a man should be forgiven any idiocy if only he is sincere. Having known more than my share of sincerely stupid people, and a few idiots, especially in the church, I am not inclined to seek a hearing for these views on any ground except the tantalizing possibility that they may be an inevitable, necessary, and desirable consequence of God's Presence in and for the world, instead of in church.

When I began writing this book several years ago, I was working as a local pastor in a Presbyterian church in New York City. Along with a couple of hundred other ordained Presbyterian ministers, I held membership in an organization called the Presbytery of New York City. During the final two years that I worked in New York City I talked, not casually but seriously, about the problems of ministry with perhaps forty or fifty men who like myself served churches there. These talks were not organized or directed. They just happened, in ways common to men who work together, serve on committees together, see one another's families, and try to meet for lunch as often as possible.

In this group of forty or fifty ordained ministers there were at least ten or twelve who wanted very much to support their families by working in a secular occupation, but who did not take that step because, as children say in one of their best games, it is a "giant step." In the past few years, seven of my own personal friends among the clergy—not in the group just mentioned—have actually taken that giant step. All seven by any reasonable and generally accepted standard of judgment were successful and effective clergy, each one occupying a position of considerably more than average influence in the life of the church. The jobs they left behind in the church in order to pursue secular occupations were jobs thousands of clergy would be glad to have. These men have gone into a considerable variety of occupations. Joe is now an assistant to the president of a state university, in charge of relating that

118

university more responsibly to the urban setting which is its immediate environment; Fred is teaching history in a large metropolitan public school system; Carl is now serving on the staff of a major foundation, channeling its resources into the urban crisis: Manfred is heading the social services division of a large public school system; Craig is teaching philosophy and sociology in a newly formed community college whose students are mostly from deprived families in urban ghettos; Jim is working in the community affairs division of a major American industry, helping that company accept corporate responsibility for social problems; Ed is working in the financial industry in Wall Street. The names of these friends are changed, but the jobs they have gone to are real, and their vocational decisions are fraught with meaning for the future of the church.

That meaning has nothing to do with statistics. From such meager, unscientific, subjective, quasi-factual evidence, I make no statistical extrapolations. But this does not mean that what is going on in their minds and hearts is without profound import for the church. On the contrary, the groping of their spirits for a better way is of utmost significance.

Those clergy friends who have moved into secular vocations are not men who want to stop serving the church of Jesus Christ. They are not men impaled on the horns of their own unresolved emotional dilemmas. They have not lost their desire to be Christ's servants. They have not abandoned, nor do they want to abandon, their ordination vows. On the contrary, these clergy-become-laymen who live with Paul's "tent-making impulse" are, as I have known them, men who were "making a go" of the professional ministry. Joe, Fred, Carl, Manfred, Craig, Jim, and Ed all believe in God with searching insight. They are not sick of the church in the sense of wanting to run away from it; rather, they are men who long for a new freedom to serve the church. They are not emotionally crippled losers who seek escape from Christ's claim on their lives; they are men who feel the commanding dimension of that claim and

119

want to honor it in a new way. They could scarcely be more earnest about fulfilling their ordination vows but found such fulfillment impossible of attainment in the institutional church as we now have it. They are not giddy, irresponsible "young Turks," dizzied by their pursuit of the latest theological fad or life style. They are mature, responsible, loyal men disturbed, salvationally, by a vision of what the church may and can be. I believe that my friends, the secular seven, are among the first of a mighty vanguard.

But my central assertion is not about the number of such men, which no one knows. Rather, I am concerned quite directly to affirm (a) that they exist; (b) that their number is growing; (c) that their number will inevitably increase dramatically; (d) that they are very loosely held together by an intuitive awareness that the church of Christ will not be free to obey its Lord until we decide to attack the problems of professional clericalism and clerical professionalism head on. Such an attack demands that we devise ways and means of helping clergy get off the church's back, thus setting clergy free to serve Christ in the church and in the world, free to be his men at dimensions of depth now undreamed of, free to be laymen.

One such clergyman is my friend Mel; his experience is relevant because it affirms the church in a way different from the affirmation of the other seven. Mel was the full-time professional pastor of a local church until about a year ago. At that time, he became a full-time school teacher for all the reasons I have identified previously in describing "the secular seven." But in Mel's case, there is one outstanding difference, he is continuing at the same time to be the pastor of that church. The revolutionary difference is that his salary is no longer paid by the church he serves, but since his teaching commitments make major demands on his time and energy, both he and the lay officers of the church have had to work out radical redefinitions of all the basic questions about church, ministry, the gospel, and the meaning of their own lives. The radical reorientation is de-professionalizing the ministry in that parish and helping all of them become an excitingly viable Christian community of laymen liberated to be the church in dimensions of responsibility and creativity previously unknown, unexplored, undreamed of.

As the movement of clergy into secular vocations gains force, another creative exercise we shall learn to perform is the affirmation of those clergy who for years have been making their living secularly and serving a congregation more or less "on the side." I refer to many ministers of store-front or rural or inner-city congregations whose members are not financially able to support a full-time professional clergyman. Many of these men are not formally educated, some have not been to college, large numbers have not been to a seminary, and all these factors have caused us to look down on them; sometimes even the men involved demean themselves as second or third class types. We must recognize these ministries as valid. These men should be affirmed as the vanguards of a movement which now needs to be embraced and strengthened by the professional clerical and middle class lay Protestant establishment. They have led the way into God's world, sometimes without knowing it, and we need to sit at their feet, gaining courage to follow.

The de-professionalizing of the ministry by strengthening laymen to fulfill the meaning of their own lives is being helped also by those rare, brave souls in the parish ministry who make their own decisions to be free men in a local situation. I think of Gene, in a neighboring parish. At this point he is not about to move from the parish ministry into a secular vocation. But the ministry of Christ's church is being de-professionalized because Gene is secure enough within himself and has enough confidence in the lordship of Christ to set laymen in his church free for ministry. He unashamedly and joyously takes sides on the controversial issues now tearing church and society apart. At great risk to his own survival in the local parish, Gene comes down consistently on the side of openness

121

to the world and to Christ's presence in the decisive public agonies of our time. He knows that this stance alienates the establishment in his own parish setting because its purpose is to tip the scales in the power struggle going on between that establishment and the newer, younger breed of laymen who are asserting that the ministry of Christ's church was always essentially secular and worldly and nonreligious, that is, a lay ministry. Because Gene makes clear to such laymen his commitment to and confidence in them, they are really taking over in that parish. Moreover, such a ministry as his attracts more and more such laymen, so that the threat to Gene is reduced to manageable proportions. Gene's decision to let his own commitment to a de-professionalized, issue-oriented, controversy-affirming, secularly shaped ministry carry him wherever it may, with no particular anxiety to prearrange the falling of the chips in a way that would shore up his own personal security, has made Gene a free man. Freedom is always intrinsically beautiful and powerful; it tends to set others free. Across the country I believe there are growing numbers of free spirits like Gene, who have not yet taken the giant step, but who are "preparing the way of the Lord" with the authenticity of their own personal commitment to the possibility that they may well be working themselves out of their jobs.

All the foregoing real-life examples underscore what I propose as a prime article of Christian faith for our time: that the secularizing processes now shaking the foundations of the institutional church—processes too many Christians have piously deplored—are not evil but good. They are God's doing. It is clear that the church must affirm the movement of clergy into secular occupations as not only inevitable but also good, good in the seminal sense of its being an actual historic work of God's Holy Spirit in Christ, good in the sense that clergy are becoming laymen. For man come of age in a church come of age in a world come of age, that is, in a time of personal, ecclesiastical, and secular maturity such as the one we are now entering, this movement is to be understood not as curse but blessing, not as a sign of failure but of triumph, not as evidence of God's death, or man's death, or the church's death, but as a sign and seal of Life—life in God, life in man, life in the church, life in the world. True life. Life abundant. Life in a Risen Christ. A mature doctrine of the Resurrection will, at bare minimum, make the church consciously and gratefully part of this movement; in Christ we shall not ignore, resist, or demean it.

If significant numbers of thoughtful Christians could see it that way, a major task during the next twenty-five or fifty years would be the creation of some new institutional machinery. Many private, secular foundations must be established to help clergy make the transition from their present positions in the professional ministry to new jobs in the secular world. The work of such foundations could center around a few basic areas of concern:

1. *Finding* the clergy who feel the impulse to change their vocation.
2. *Counseling* with them to be sure their vocational desire is truly for greater freedom in the service of the church and the world.
3. *Retraining and reeducating* these men for secular jobs, and placing them in such jobs.
4. *Financing* these clergy and their families during the transition period so they will not be subjected to needless and nonproductive deprivation.
5. *Guiding* local churches in the transition period so they and their secularly employed ministers could effectively implement the whole complex of new relationships and responsibilities, de-professionalizing the ministry together.
6. *Encouraging* and helping theological seminaries and other church structures to affirm this movement and be part of

123

it by enabling them to effect the upheaval in theological education whose basic principles were described earlier in this chapter.

It is informative to ponder a few of the financial, psychological, and spiritual implications of such possible developments. For instance, it is clear that additional millions of dollars would be available to the church every year, even at present levels of giving. For the annual cost of clergy salaries, pensions, allowances, etc., which consume 40 to 75 percent of the local church income, would be there to be spent for other purposes. Moreover, this would be accomplished without depriving the church of leadership. To be sure, local churches would be deprived of ordained clergy as we have, until now, understood their roles and responsibilities. But the clergy would be there and available in a new way, as laymen. For if there is truth in what I have written about the desire of clergymen to be more free in serving the church, then it is not quixotic to suggest that many of these same men would want to go on being leaders in local churches. Within the limits of their time and strength they would continue to do so.

The basic economic-psychological-theological difference would be that these men would offer their services to local congregations, and as theological consultants to vocationally oriented groups of laymen, and in many other leadership capacities, on exactly the same basis that other laymen now offer their services to the church, that is, without being paid for them. To be sure, those freely offered services would be limited by the demands of their secular jobs, just as laymen are now similarly limited. In consequence, clergy-become-laymen and laymen would have to arrive at revolutionary understandings of "the work of the church"—what it is, what priorities it affirms, what presuppositions direct it and, above all, where the "work" of the church occurs. Much that we now consider important or essential would have to go. The church would never look the same again, because the ministry would be de-professionalized and made primarily the ministry of laymen.

The whole process, though extremely difficult and upsetting to many, though it would take many years to accomplish broadly, would finally be immensely life-giving for the whole church. And even more, life-giving for the whole world. For at all organizational levels—local parish, regional bodies, national and international boards and agencies—one of the principal sources of unproductive and paralyzing institutionalism, with all its concomitant wastages of money, ideas, and men, is the simple fact that the institution now has so many of us clergy on its back. Honest men know there is probably no institution in American society where Parkinson's Law works with more lethal effect than in the church, precisely because the whole deadly process is alleged to be "religious" and "spiritual" and, what is even less credible, "Christian."

For us clergy to admit this to ourselves and to those fine, thoughtful laymen who are in every church, and for us to begin doing something about it together, however cautiously, would be a fantastically renewing action. As the new relationships emerged, undreamed-of dimensions of mutual trust, understanding, and respect would grow. Not only would laymen listen to such clergy-become-laymen more attentively because they worked in the laymen's world of secular reality; they would also listen more attentively and respond to such leaders more faithfully because their services to the church came at the same price as their own—free. And the clergy-become-laymen would be liberated because the ministry of the church would be fully, freely, and steadily turned over to laymen.

There are additional considerations relative to finance. Clergy making their living in the secular world would be making decent livings in many instances for the first time in their lives. Many would be able and gladly willing to give money to the church alive, and to do this generously from the resources of their own increased economic productivity. This complex movement will be so cleansing and empowering for the whole church as to produce annual additions to church income staggering to the wildest imagination, making our present budgetary allocations look like skimpy children's allowances. New resources of money will spring from the Church's felt gratitude for life in death.

In confining this chapter to the discussion of theological education and a movement of clergy into secular occupations, I am not guilty of oversimplification. For I am keenly aware that there are many other equally important and dynamic forces which are now, and will be in the decades to come, creatively at work in the life of the church. I am also aware of the fact that I have made no effort here to spell out the implications of what I have said for such vital areas as worship, Christian education of children, Christian education of adults, the use of church lands and buildings, Christian family life, the work of administrators in the church, to mention only a few central and abiding concerns. Additionally, I am aware that the revolution in theological education and the movement of clergy into secular occupations are long-range goals for the church. Admittedly, I have not pointed to detailed ways and means of getting to these goals. Mapping out such details and implementing them at all levels of church life will take years, decades perhaps generations, although some specifics have already become obvious.

I have refrained from major discussion of such specifics because to do so at this time and in this place would serve only to befog the issue. Something else must come first: church members must be engaged, as they are not now engaged, in a mighty struggle with the revolutionary questions raised in this field manual, not as polite debaters but as men and women whose churches have been largely abandoned by the living God, and who are therefore determined to conduct a revolution in those churches.

Those revolutionary questions include the following:

1. Is it true that our willingness to be profoundly disturbed, personally and institutionally, has in our time become the prerequisite of Christian salvation?
2. Have we lost Christ in the church because we have transformed our churches into spiritual prisons which lock men away from the world where he is present?
3. In our time, has the church become Christ's principal antagonist?
4. Is "the open ministry" as described in this field manual the one to which God is now calling the whole church?
5. Have we made our life and practice in the church a massive denial of the open ministry? Is the resulting professionalism in our churches a death-dealing plague?
6. Is the call to implement the open ministry on a massive scale an invitation to laymen to discover the very meaning of their lives not only as church members, but also as human beings?
7. Is personal salvation through confrontation with God-in-Christ produced primarily through inextricable personal involvement in the renewal and restoration of the human community?
8. Is God-in-Christ calling all Christians, but especially laymen, to make politics the language of evangelism?
9. Must we have a revolution in theological education? Is the revolution in theological education proposed here a responsible revolution? Is it the necessary and finally inevitable consequence of all theological insights centering on God's presence in and for the world? However upsetting and disturbing for all of us, is such a revolution right for the church and for the world? Is it God's will?

127

10. Is the movement of clergy into secular occupations the wave of the future? Should the church be for it or against it? Is talk of such a movement hot air or the "wind of the Spirit"?

11. Is Holy Scripture still being written? Is God, by the power of his Spirit, creating a new Bible? Should the canon be officially reopened? Is it now a major task of laymen to discern the written Word of God in a staggering multiplicity of secular texts and contexts and, by so doing, to intensify greatly the dynamics of revolution in the church?

12. Is "adulthood" what is really happening to us? Are we actually growing out of our adolescent spiritual need for much, if not most, of what the church has called "religion"? Is "religionless Christianity" the work of the Holy Spirit? Should laymen resist its growth or yield to it and permit its dynamic power to carry the church across the threshold of revolutionary consent?

13. Is the Protestant ethic, with its emphasis on intense individualism, a denial of Christian community? Is that ethic, elevated to the status of controlling myth, holding the church back from that future which God has prepared for the church? Who should lead the way in an effort to recognize that ethic's demonic potential?

14. Can the present polarization in the church be accepted and used as a means of grace and growth? Can we learn, in the church, to affirm conflict and to manage it creatively? What insights, skills, risks, and commitments will this require? Is the gathering storm in the churches the wind of the Spirit? Is survival the overriding issue?

The last question creates an opportunity to explain what I mean in calling for a mighty struggle with these revolutionary enquiries. I do not mean that the church should now organize a massive collection of study groups to explore the arguments on all sides of these questions. It is too late in the

128

day for that. Such a polite debating-society approach will produce nothing but death for the church. *What I do mean and clearly reaffirm is that the answers to these questions are now known, and that the only hope for the church is through acts of faith and commitment which will give personal and institutional validity to those known answers.* Returning for the moment to the polarization between John and Bill, I want to affirm that the Lord Jesus is calling on us to take sides with Bill, for the sufficient reason that Bill answers these inescapable questions in a particular way: We must put up or shut up. These questions are the seas of God's creation where those called "fishers of men" must, at long last, fish or cut bait. My purpose is to catalyze that crucial process of decision-making by encouraging a revolution in the church, a revolution which asks men and women to deal with our present desperate polarization by taking sides with Bill, that is, through acts of risk in commitment and commitment in risk, acts by men come of age through a church come of age in a world come of age.

In taking such a controversial stance, I wish to make it clear that revolutionaries are not anti-institutional just for the sake of being so. No responsible man is. On the contrary, it should be manifest to every reader that what I have proposed all along the way are alternative institutions. There are no apologies for that. It is at once inevitable and wise that Christian faith and life shall have institutional expression. Any institution, old or new, can become an object of idolatry, an impediment to witness, a barrier to mission, a frustration rather than a fulfillment of purpose. Of course. But that ever present possibility is not germane at this crucial moment in history.

The germane consideration now is that those institutional expressions of Christianity which we have, in fact, worked out and which do, in fact, constitute the substance of church life today have become historical objects of massive idolatrous attachment. Mainly for this reason the church has in many minds, especially those of young people, become exhibit A for those who claim that God is dead. This indictment is not rendered less valid by a creative ministry here and there, a renewed congregation here and there, a new thrust here and there. There are exceptions to prove every rule. And these signs of new life, of which we all know and for which we all are grateful, are exactly that. They are flashes of lightning illumining the main body of damaging evidence. That evidence is the whole complex of idolatrous attachments, habits, and priorities which have grown up around and finally become the institutional church as we know it.

In a wider context, comprehending the whole of our society, Erich Fromm has, without realizing it, brilliantly analyzed the present desperate tragedy of the church in a passage every Christian should memorize as an exercise in Christian devotion.

What is it that makes a society viable, allowing it to respond to change? There is no simple answer, but clearly the society must above all be able to discriminate its primary values from its secondary values and institutions. This is difficult because secondary systems generate values of their own, which come to appear as essential as the human and social needs which brought them into being. As people's lives become intertwined with institutions, organizations, life styles, forms of productions and consumption, etc., men become willing to sacrifice themselves and others for the works of their own hands, to transform their own creatures into idols and to worship these idols. Furthermore, institutions generally resist change, and thus men who are fully committed to institutions are not free to anticipate change. The problem, then, for a society such as ours today, is whether men can rediscover the basic human and social values of our civilization and withdraw their allegiance, not to say their worship, from those of their institutional (or ideological) values which have become obstructive.[*]

Sometimes in this life we have to honor the prerogatives of death. Sometimes we are required to let that which is dying die in order that something new may be born. Not only

[*] Erich Fromm, *May Man Prevail?* (Garden City, N. Y.: Doubleday & Co., 1961), p. 7.

in the New Testament, but also in an honest reading of what we actually go through, there is unyielding insistence that we do not live in Christ until first we die with him. Death precedes resurrection, and there is no neat way of avoiding, altering, or changing that sequence. "The Old Being has the mark of disintegration and death. The New Being puts a new mark over the old one. Out of disintegration and death something is born of eternal significance. That which is immersed in dissolution emerges in a New Creation." [4]

In that New Creation all men and women will be ministers and missionaries in the specific sense that all will be involved in and committed to the secular world as those who know what their lives are for, that is, for service. Through its individual members that New Creation will form massive interlocking alliances with the power structures of the world, not for the purpose of dominating or controlling them. Rather, the purpose will be to transform them into instruments of service for other men, especially at those points where those others feel pain. In that New Creation Christian laymen will create a truly secular ecumenicity, bringing into being joint actions and strategies with the self-contained worlds of business, education, science, politics, industry, law, organized labor, medicine, and the arts, to the end that these disciplines and enterprises shall respond more freely to the needs, longings, hopes, fears, and pains of all men. In that New Creation resurrection power will not be frail myth or insubstantial hope, but Reality known, verified, and given institutional expression as the Power which sets us free. Free to find our lives in a living Christ. Free, genuinely free to give those lives away for anybody who may need them. Free to be in the world. Free to be human.

The deepest dimensions of that freedom are measured inwardly, and we must explore them now lest the revolutionary community be demeaned as having no inner life. For those

[4] Paul Tillich, *The New Being* (New York: Charles Scribner's Sons, 1955), p. 24.

radical changes now occurring in the church are not simplistic reruns of the Social Gospel, and radicals in the church are not just social activists. It behooves us to understand that the inwardness of the revolutionary community is genuine and therefore powerful.

IX   The Inwardness
of the Revolutionary Community

Irresistible and finally irrepressible changes of a radical nature are generating in the church because a new inwardness is emerging among committed laymen like Bill, and because that inwardness is genuine. In Central Church, Montclair, Bill is a force to be reckoned with because his inwardness is authentic. Frightened people criticize him for not valuing what they call "the fundamentals": prayer, worship, Bible study, and a vigorous enthusiasm for hallowed priority systems in the church and in the world. These are fair, accurate criticisms of Bill if "the inner life" and "the spiritual life" are defined in traditional terms. But they are unfair and inaccurate in whatever measure they imply that Bill is a stranger to inwardness, for he surely is not. On the contrary, he is one of the most interior persons in the church and community. And no one —least of all John—can write him off easily because even those who, like John, disagree vehemently with Bill, sense the authenticity of his inner life. That inwardness creates force and power, for it gives Bill depth. This fact—that he is not a surface skimmer—makes Bill and his fellow-seekers a creative, not-to-be-ignored, disturbing, change-producing presence in the church. Not just in Central Church, but all over America such laymen, nourished by the new inwardness, are becoming what I choose to call "the revolutionary community." Their significance lies in the fact that they are confronting the whole church, especially in the local parish, with something much more formidable than the Social Gospel. For their inwardness is more deeply rooted than was that of an earlier generation of liberals.

An example of what I mean is provided by those laymen who in recent years have been trained for mission through the work of the Ecumenical Institute. Since its founding in 1954 as a division of the Church Federation of Greater Chicago, the

133

Ecumenical Institute has been one of the most issue-oriented, socially activist influences on the American church scene. Through hundreds of staff people who are products of the Institute's training emphasis on local congregational renewal, scores of parishes and thousands of laymen have been made aware of the opportunities present, the knowledge required, and the skills needed for changing local church structures into radical mission tools. If one looked only at the surface of such efforts one might assume that they were contemporary versions of programs devised by the old social-gospelers.

But the relevant consideration, indeed, the very core of difference between the two movements, is the ever growing inwardness of contemporary social activists—not an inwardness which waters down or compromises concern for Christian involvement in the secular world, but rather an inwardness from which that involvement draws its strength. It is indeed significant that the June 1970 issue of the Institute's journal *Image* is wholly devoted to "The Solitary Life of the Secular Religious." The introduction puts it this way:

The publication of this issue of *Image* is a sign of a major turning point in the life and work of the staff of The Ecumenical Institute and in the course of the Church in the twentieth century. In the last two years the staff of the Institute, as a research body on behalf of the whole Church, has been struggling with the implications of the global cultural crisis as it has been illuminated by recent events that have shattered the composure of every human being who is sensitive to what is going on. Such events have signaled the collapse of the optimistic social activism that characterized the mood of the Church in the sixties. . . . Today the man of faith is raising again the deep questions of human destiny that drive him back to reflect on his interior solitary existence. . . . The deep question of what it means to create a new secular piety for the twentieth century religious man has compelled the research staff of The Ecumenical Institute to undertake a depth examination of the devotional life of the individual, or the solitary religious practices of meditation, contemplation, and prayer.[1]

[1] *Image,* Journal of the Ecumenical Institute, No. 9, June 1970.

That statement is not an isolated phenomenon. It is not something I affirm about a small, limited group. Rather, I offer it as a profound symbol because of that to which it points, namely, the emergence in the whole church of the new inwardness, the new secular piety, the kind and quality of inner life now being nourished by secular human commitments to a truly sovereign Christ.

I shall validate the judgment that this new inwardness is stronger and deeper than any that characterized the old Social Gospel movement by describing it in some detail. Because the new inwardness is developing in a framework of insights and institutions still in the process of formation, my description will not produce a tidy, finished system and will, of necessity, be informed by the ambiguities intrinsic to the formation of any new discipline. But the description will at least sustain the judgment I have made and spotlight the superficiality of those who maintain that "the revolutionary community" is shallow, or unspiritual, or unconcerned about personal relationships to Christ.

It is integral to the method of the new inwardness to make a careful distinction between what is personal and what is private, a distinction of which the old, outworn pieties were scarcely aware. This distinction is reflected in an announcement sent to the members of St. Paul's Episcopal Church, Englewood, New Jersey, inviting them to participate in its adult education program:

All we want you to do here is to enter into the discipline of this operation on a personal basis so that it might be possible for you to discover some things about yourself which are "religiously" significant for you in terms of your own life, but which are, nevertheless, privately your own concern. In order to accomplish what we have to do, we feel that we have to find some way of communicating with one another on a personal and not private basis, and so, we will attempt to find those symbolic reflections within each of our lives which we can talk about generally, since they affect us all, and yet which we cannot talk about privately, since for each one of us they will be different.

The new inwardness seeks and cultivates those disciplines of study, thought, discussion, reflection, and action which are personal because in them we find ourselves as persons related to the basic issues of human existence. In so doing, the new inwardness does not permit us to indulge the corrupting luxuries of endless navel gazing sometimes cultivated by process-oriented efforts at self-discovery, nor does it permit, bless, and sanctify the shallow, saccharine, and sometimes egomaniacal sentimentality which for generations has been the nearly universal stock-in-trade of traditional understandings of Christian inwardness.

The new inwardness is personal without being private and takes far more cues from actual human experience than it does from doctrines or systems of theology, or even from principles of biblical interpretation. The raw material of the new inwardness is not dogma or theology or a philosophical world view, but rather the stubbornly elusive stuff or our own daily lives. It does not start from lofty principles but from the awesome mystery of what we actually go through as human beings. Therefore the language of the new inwardness tends to be fragmentary, unsystematic, and warmly human. Both its language and its method have about them not the odor of some dull theological abstraction, but the lusty smell of life as we actually know it, live it, feel it, laugh it, and cry it into being.

Michael Novak illumines this emphasis on experience by suggesting that for Christians it is not so important to ask what it means to be a Christian as it is to ask what it means to be a human being:

In principle, it seems good to attend more closely to our actual experience as Christians than to theories, formulas or doctrines which purport to articulate and to direct that experience. For experience is in principle richer, more complex, and more full of novelty than limited conceptual schemes can compass. Fresh attention to experience is a major source of newer and more accurate formulas. . . . Theory . . . is for the sake of life, and sometimes the lure of life exceeds what present theories can handle. Ours seems to be such a time.[2]

Indeed, ours is such a time, a time in which we are becoming more deeply and creatively Christian precisely because we are yielding to the sternly beautiful pressures of the humanist impulse, the impulse which helps us embrace a deeply creative paradox, namely, that "the purpose of a Christian life is not to become more Christian but less so; not to become more parochial and special but less so. The purpose of a Christian life is to become all that a human being can become, to become more fully human." [3]

With humanness at once its method and its goal, the new inwardness is creating a new community of faith, of insight, of purpose, and of action, a new Christian community, if you will, a revolutionary community of persons discovering one another across traditional walls and through time-honored barriers of incommunicability. Recently I spoke with a man who is twenty-eight and a woman who is twenty-six. We had made an appointment to discuss their forthcoming marriage, but for the first hour of our talk we never mentioned marriage. The prospective groom is a professional writer. We began with that eminently human bit of data, we discussed his writing, then moved into a discussion of their hopes, convictions, and commitments. He stands outside of and detached from the institutional church. But as we probed the nature of his commitment as a writer, we made the rather amazing discovery that he as a secular writer and I as a minister—he who stands in a state of creative disaffiliation from the church and I who stand inside the church as an institution—do, in fact, belong to a new community. It is a community of men and women bound together by the very human values which the new inwardness cultivates and discerns. This revolutionary community is vague,

[2] Michael Novak, "Human First, Christian Second," *The Christian Century*, June 19, 1968, p. 815.

[3] *Ibid.*, p. 818.

elusive, ill-structured, and loosely organized, to be sure, but still, for all that, profoundly real. It is a community which finds its members and whose members mysteriously find one another inside and outside the institutions of religion, a community which draws its members from the Protestant churches, the Roman Catholic Church, the Jewish synagogues, and also from those who have no relationship to any religious institution, that is, from agnostics and atheists and secularists, men and women from anywhere and everywhere who are yielding to the humanist impulse. As we yield to that impulse, we discover our common commitment to the restoration of the human community, and as we deepen that commitment, fulfilling it in responsible social action, we do in very truth experience not only our own and one another's inner depths, but also the depths of him whose commitment to the healing of the human community had no limits. "As I read with attention," writes Novak in that same essay,

the works of writers—Albert Camus, Bertrand Russell, Walter Kaufmann, Sidney Hook, Jean-Paul Sarte, Gerhard Szczesny, *et al.*—who describe themselves as atheists or even as anti-Christian, I often find in them the spiritual kinship that I find in some Christian writers but not in others; I feel closer to them than to many Christian theologians. . . . When they state the values to which they give primary allegiance, I find myself making the same sort of appropriation . . . as I make with Christian writers of comparable stature. These atheists often seem closer in their perceptions to various insights of the Gospels than some Christian theologians are. In brief, the experiences of everyday living and everyday reflection seem to show that the same graces of understanding and loving which are touchstones of a Christian presence are manifested prodigally among those who are not Christians. Grace, wrote Georges Bernanos, is everywhere.[4]

If that sounds to some like an unforgivable watering down of the historic Christian faith to the weak, tasteless wine of pallid humanism, my response is this: One of our options as Christians is to affirm a Christ so truly sovereign, so truly Lord,

4 *Ibid.*, p. 815.

that he doesn't have to be transported anywhere. He simply has to be discerned where he really is: everywhere and anywhere, in all history and all culture. I do, indeed, confess and affirm that Christ, a Christ who cannot be and is not boxed up inside the neat little categories we call "religious" and "spiritual." The new inwardness makes that affirmation without patronizing our brothers in Christ who are Catholics and Jews and secularists and agnostics, for we affirm that sovereignty by sitting at their feet to practice the Presence of a Lord not confined to the constructs in which we have tried to encapsulate him; at their feet we touch and handle the inexhaustible riches in Christ which have been concealed from us by our captivity to traditional understandings of inwardness.

As it leads us out of that captivity, the new inwardness is teaching us to take risks we have been unable or unwilling to take before—risks in thought, risks in discipline, in service, in commitment, in love. Robert Dodds illumines the nature of those risks in an essay called "The Meaning of Membership":

Let me tell you a story told to me long ago by a friend. Before World War II he did not consider himself a Christian, but he was fascinated with Christianity and wanted to study it. As a part of his graduate course he went to France to study with a distinguished Protestant faculty. His arrival in France happened to coincide with Hitler's occupation of that land. The faculty with which he wanted to work was forced to go underground, meeting in private homes and church basements, wherever they could find asylum. Every night, he said, the faculty and students met for a common meal and for prayers. Periodically there was an empty place at the table. No one knew whether the missing member had been murdered or detained or shipped off to a concentration camp. In that strained situation, no one thought to ask my friend whether he was a Christian. He had chosen to affiliate with a community in peril. Everyone assumed that he belonged. This is an approach to membership we should remember. Under conditions of persecution, whoever chooses to act like the persecuted ones is likely to be considered a member.[5]

[5] Robert C. Dodds, "The Meaning of Membership," *The Christian Century*, September 11, 1968, p. 1136.

The new inwardness brings men and women into voluntary commitment to "a community in peril." And the opposite is also true; commitment to a community in peril deepens the new inwardness. In both instances, the centrally experienced reality is risk. It is this perception and a growing readiness to take grave personal and institutional risks which enables practitioners of the new inwardness to understand that one learns the game, as Winston Churchill observed, by risking more than he can possibly afford to lose. Practitioners of the new inwardness tend to gamble in that way. We do so knowing that there is never a built-in assurance of winning.

There cannot be, for the new inwardness of the revolutionary community is most profoundly characterized by the crucial distinction its adherents make between "Christian faith and life" on the one hand, and "Christian religion" on the other. Throughout this field manual I have alluded to that crucial distinction. Now it is all-important to make it explicit, for that distinction, with its personal and institutional consequences, constitutes the very core of the new inwardness.

Christian religion is an intricately elaborate human construct whose ingredients are sociological, cultural, psychological, aesthetic, anthropological, political, economic, and artistic in nature. In its most refined expressions, human religion is an exquisite accomplishment. But its exquisiteness does not change its fundamental function of providing response and ministry to the universal human need for escape from the ambiguity, the tragedy, the raw, bleeding pain of human life. Life, real life which God indwells and in which He is known and loved, life as reality is pain and creates a universal human longing for relief from pain. It was in the context of that need and of religion's universal ministrations to it that Karl Marx said religion is the "opiate of the people." So it is. For it is Christian religion, not Christian faith and life, which we have institutionalized and enthroned to power in the church.

As regards the Christian brand of human religion, what has happened historically, at least in Western civilization, is that

140

we have used that very human construct to isolate and insulate man from life and from the living Lord Jesus Christ by involving him in an infinitely complex ministration to his felt need to run away from life, to retreat from reality, to hide from God, from other men, and from his own inner self. Through the Christian brand of human religion we have taught ourselves to live in a world of theological-spiritual-metaphysical fantasy, and in so doing created our most sophisticated death option.

However elaborately exquisite and intellectually competent our rationale for the Christian brand of religion, still the hard-core truth of the whole matter is that Christian religion over against Christian faith and life is an instrumentality of death; it helps man to move toward death-in-life for the simple reason that the living God who is the source of all aliveness dwells in a basically different, opposite dimension of experience—the nonreligious, unreligious, secular, worldly dimension. He dwells in life itself, human life in all its sanity and madness, all its courage and fear, its grandeur and misery, its hope and despair, in all its glory and degradation, all its excitement, boredom, suffering, defeat, victory, its heartache, its enigmatic quality of engulfing and sometimes terrifying mystery. In the depths of that whole uncertain mystery of reality which is human life is God-in-Christ. But also in the depths of that aliveness is the certainty of pain and therefore the raw material of man's longing not to be hurt.

So the centuries of man's infatuation with religion passed, centuries in which the church taught man not to be Christian, but to be religious. That long historical process extending through generations came to consummate expression for me two years ago when I read this letter a week before Easter:

Dear Dr. Huber:
I am registering a strong protest against all these new ideas of growth, etc. Please—may we not once in a while hear a sermon that concerns itself with *religion?* How about some revered, old, and cherished faith in our country?
Sincerely. . . .

141

When I first read that plea for more "religion" in the church, let me tell you how I felt and still often feel. I wanted to rush up to the man who wrote it, put my arms around him, and say: "I hear you, friend. I hear you, because that's what I want, too. Like you, I don't want to be Christian. I just want to be religious. Like you, I want to come to church and not be hurt anymore. Like you, I don't want to hear one more word about the urban crisis. Like you, I want to come to church not to find God and Christ and reality and Life, but to find religion and be at peace. Like you, I've had enough of the storm and I want shelter. Like you, I want to retreat, to escape, to run away from life and reality and the world, even if it is the only world there ever was or is or will be. Like you, I want religion, because the reality of life is more than I can handle, and like you, with you, I want to die. I do not condemn you, friend, and I do not judge you, because I hear and understand you, and something way down deep inside me wants exactly the kind of religion you want."

That is one part of my answer to his letter. But, in addition to that plea for his understanding compassion, there is something else I wanted to say to the man who wrote it: "Way down deep inside you and me there is, in addition to the longing for a religion that will insulate us from reality, a deeper, sturdier longing for life itself, an insatiable thirst for reality, an ineluctably passionate yearning to move away from death toward life by moving away from Christian religion toward true Christian faith and life. And that longing is there in us, my friend, because you and I are not made for death. We are made for Life, not death but Life is our destiny. Death, including the death we embrace inside the boundaries of religion, is the enemy. And that enemy has been overcome. In religion there is death. But in Christ there is no death. For the victory is won, friend, even the victory over death in its most sophisticated form, which is our religion, yes, even that victory is sealed for you and me. Not even Christian religion is strong enough to extinguish our lust for life."

Evidence of that victory arrived in the mail a few days later in the following letter, written by an elderly member of Central Church.

> Dear Dr. Huber:
> Having received and read the "the very long letter" (the "very long letter" was from the Session of Central Church about a series of "Urban Crisis Observances" in which we were then engaged) several times, I even wish it were longer, and that I could think of more ways to help with the work. I enclose a check as my "Urban Crisis Offering," to be used as you think best. . . .

The letter went on to suggest one or two specific additional ways in which the writer might be able to help and closed with these words: "I am sorry I cannot attend more occasions at the church at present, but I am proud to be a member where so much is accomplished. Sincerely. . . ." Enclosed was a check for $150 for an Urban Crisis Offering which was one in a series of corporate responses the Church made that spring to the situation in Newark. In itself, one such offering might be deemed insignificant, but symbolically it was of great importance because it pointed out the direction in which the practice of the new inwardness had already begun to move Central Church. It was a foretaste of things to come, and for many it was a bitter taste. As one church in the Presbytery, we gave $3,500 on that occasion and united it with gifts from other churches, so that the Presbytery of Newark was able to make a gift of $25,000, with no strings of middle-class accountability attached, to a secular group of black leaders in the Newark ghetto. In a crucial sense it is inaccurate to assert that there were no strings attached; for the influence of the new inwardness in the congregation had made crystal clear the profound sense in which there *were* strings attached—strings of love, respect, and confidence which bound us to those leaders in common commitment to the restoration of that broken human community. The emerging new inwardness in Central Church had illumined the meaning of the gift: our soldarity with Newark's Central Ward, and the dissolution of old, cherished boundaries between that inner-city part of our common community and the suburban part called Montclair.

Along with other more significant corporate responses to the Urban Crisis, it alienated many of our members. It was part of a long, painful process in which members transferred to other churches, dropped out, conducted an economic boycott by reducing dramatically or eliminating entirely their pledges of money to Central Church. For a whole congregation, that year was the beginning of a long, dark night of the soul which had its issue in the intense polarization described in the first Chapter about John and Bill. That dark night of the soul came to us, as a people, because the practice of the new inwardness among a small but growing number simply would not permit us, individually or corporately, to run away from reality and seek shelter in "religion." During the long, critical months which followed, practitioners of the new inwardness knew that we had come to a decisive turning point and were determined that we would not turn back. It was they who kept Central heading into the very center of the gathering storm. The mood and method, the assumptions and techniques, the understandings and priorities of the new inwardness as I have described them helped and forced us to ask the basic question about Christian "religion" as opposed to Christian "faith and life." That seminal query has never been more precisely articulated than in these words: "Do we affirm the Easter faith in our time by insisting that God raised Jesus from the dead or by daring to risk ourselves in the confidence that God will raise us from the dead?" [6] The answer became clear in the measure that we did not seek shelter from the reality-storm: The Resurrection is affirmed by risking ourselves and our religious institutions in the confidence that God will raise

[6] C. Ebb Munden III, "Renewal of the Church," *motive* magazine, January 1963, p. 3.

us from the deadness of Christian religion into the aliveness of Christian faith and life.

In what, precisely, does that risk consist? Practitioners of the new inwardness make this final wager, play for keeps, in the measure of our willingness to throw away the crutches of religion. That throw-away is the incontestable evidence of faith. It affirms that the apostle Paul was right in the first century, that Augustine was right in the fourth century, that Martin Luther was right in the sixteenth century, and that Karl Barth was right in the twentieth century when they, in their historical contexts, insisted that the real and only question about resurrection was not whether God raised Jesus from the dead, but whether we have enough faith in Christ, here and now, to place ourselves in those positions of personal and institutional risk where he may resurrect us from all our love affairs with death. The core truth is now what it has always been: the just shall live, not by religion but by faith, and faith alone.

To be justified by faith today is to affirm Christ as alive by affirming life itself. Faith is the act of laying aside everything in religion which does not inextricably implicate and enmesh us in the blinding hope and agony of life itself, the life of reality in ourselves and in the world. Faith makes open sieves of brick church walls so that the world itself, the real and only world there is, flows in and out of our worship, prayers, study, planning, music, structures, our everything, with the regularity and power of the secular tide itself, the tide of life, the tide of reality, not only when it is ebbing and flowing with calmness and order, but equally and more so when that tide has been whipped into raging storms which threaten to destroy us.

The new inwardness invites us to move outside the religious ghettos our churchly institutions have become and discern Christ's presence in city slums and suburban towns, in executive suites, in political caucuses, in the board rooms of banks and businesses, in cocktail lounges and clubhouses and athletic fields, in concert halls and flophouses, in college classrooms and gin mills, in operating rooms, police stations, in

145

country clubs and living rooms and family quarrels, in cabinet meetings and school boards, and ski slopes and bedrooms, and battlefields and marches for peace, in riots and demonstrations, in bridge parties, in family joys and tragedies, in political campaigns, in Lincoln Center and the East Village, in the bums of the bowery and the matrons of Park Avenue, in children starving by the millions and in the abundance of an affluent society, in science and technology, in courts of law, in schools and factories and local elections, in laser beams and radio signals from other sentient beings out in space, in disease and research, in medicine and law and crime, in love and violence, in the whole enigmatic, uncertain, hopeful, and frightening mystery which is life, life itself in the world, Christian reality.

Having discerned there, in reality, the Presence of our living Lord, the new inwardness bestirs us to bring all that reality of his world back inside church walls, and to mix it inextricably with everything we do and think and plan in our Christian fellowship, so that our worship, our music, our liturgies, our study of his word in the Bible, our study of his word in the opened canon of contemporary writings of all kinds, our budgets, buildings, and structures for mission become living testimony to the fact that we are no longer slaves to religion but free men, free in Christ, free in obedience, free to affirm Christ by affirming reality, free to move away from death by abandoning religion for a life of faith in the living Christ, free to affirm this present year of our Lord:

I cannot imagine a more enjoyable time to be a Christian except possibly in the first few centuries of the Church. For while the great holocaust is sweeping away much that is beautiful and all that is safe and comfortable and unquestioned, it is relieving us of mounds of Christian bric-a-brac as well, and the liberation is unspeakable. Stripped of our nonsense we may almost be like the early Christians painting their primitive symbols on the walls of the catacombs—the fish, the grapes, the loaves of bread, the cross,

146

the monogram of Christ—confident that in having done so they had described the necessities of life.[7]

That is what all this turbulence in the church and in the world is about: It is a new day in which we are moving from death to life, a new era of creativity in which we are being born again.

Advocates and practitioners of the new inwardness know that there will, of course, be some skirmishing in the boondocks but also that the battle is won. That victory is what the new inwardness affirms, the story it tells. In essence, it is a story about being free:

> —free to declare the end of one era, the era of Christian religion, a religion which God used because he is so alive in Christ that not even our religion could finally kill him;
>
> —free also to participate in the beginning of a new era, the era of Christian faith and life;
>
> —free to stop being religious and to start being Christian;
>
> —free to move from the edge of disaster to the edge of an incredibly beautiful discovery.

[7] Monica Furlong, *The Guardian*, January 11, 1963.

X   On the Edge of Discovery

There was a time not too many years ago when I did not believe about the church, the ministry, the Christian faith, and the Christian life those things I have written here. I did not believe them for the reason that there is something truly infinite about man's capacity for self-deception.

Claiming my own finite share of that infinite capacity, I used it as the foundation material for a whole career in the Christian ministry. On that foundation I built a superstructure of very "religious" activity and accomplishment. That superstructure was beautiful in some ways, utilitarian in many. It brought certain satisfactions. It had survival value for me and others. Generally it blended in with those images and understandings of Christian faith and life prevalent in the churches I served. It produced a modest degree of recognition, respect, and reward. It became a way of life. But it was all profoundly self-deceptive, for the end result was not life but death.

That whole complex superstructure of work in the Christian ministry gradually became in me the raw material of idolatry, and idolatry in turn became the raw material of death. My life in the church and my work in the church were idolatrously death-dealing in the sense that my most religious efforts in the building of that superstructure were the ones in which I somehow knew, however inarticulately, that aliveness was being drained away, aliveness in God and in my own being. By some sort of strangely reverse English, I experienced that law of diminishing returns within which religion and idolatry and death become synonymous.

At a thousand places along the way I began to move from death to life, that is, from "religion" as most Christian clergy and laymen think of it today to a whole new set of understandings of the church, the ministry, and Christian faith. It has been a long, painful journey most of which I have not wanted to take. But it has been nourished and sustained by an ineluctable joy, for such joy belongs to life, not death. Sensing, as I do, that the journey has only begun, I sometimes wonder where it will end. Not often do I so speculate, for in the lives of all of us the answer to that question really belongs to God. Far more relevant in our lives is a different question: Are we learning anything genuinely worthwhile along the way, anything good enough to pass along?

In my case, the answer is yes. I have learned one lesson worth sharing. It is not a new lesson. Many learned it long ago and more thoroughly. I am a Johnny-come-lately. Maybe that is why I am equipped to teach this lesson to others, or to try. While it is not a new lesson, it is a very hard one. Not hard to learn. Not hard to understand. Just hard, very, very hard, to accept. After much reflection I have come to realize that this single lesson can be stated in seven different ways. All seven finally mean the same thing, but each produces a different shade of meaning and is, therefore, essential to the whole lesson:

I.

"Religion" is man's principal instrument of self-deception.

II.

What man, generally speaking, calls his "religion" is what he devises and constructs to insulate himself from any greater degree of contact with God and man than he, man, happens to want.

III.

In order to create the possibility of genuine fellowship between God and man and between man and man, what we must get rid of is self-deceptive "religion."

149

IV.

In the world, man's greatest problem is not war, or poverty, or hunger, or race, or anything else under the sun. Man's greatest problem is self-deceptive "religion" because it permits him to believe he is tackling those other problems (war, poverty, hunger, race, etc.) when he is, in fact, only playing with them or evading them.

V.

In the church, Christian man's greatest problem is to peel away and destroy all the layers of "religion" which are now confused with the Christian faith and the Christian life, thus making selfish and apathetic isolation from man and God difficult, if not impossible.

VI.

Institutions tend to buttress man's infinite capacity for "religious" self-deception by offering him so many good and worthy substitutes for, and evasions of, the life for others to which Christ calls every Christian and all Christians in the church.

VII.

Because "religion" is man's principal instrument of self-deception, and because in our time we have uniquely permitted the church to become an expression of man's "religion" more than we have permitted it to become an expression of Christian faith and life, Christian man resists change in the church more vehemently than he resists change in any other institution in our society. He has to, for if his "religion" goes, the last cherished barriers between himself, other men, and God are down, and he, man, is left alone with no live option except to become Christian. And who wants that?

Not many of us. Not really. In the church we resist change not only because self-deception for a long time is a very pleasant process, but also because the abandonment of self-deception brings us face to face with the unknown. The unknown is always frightening. In the church we cling to "religion" instead of to Christian faith and life because "religion" is a known quantity. "Religion" is safe. "Religion" is predictable. We know what will happen if we make commitments to "religion."

But Christian faith and life, personally embraced and institutionally expressed, are for most of us unknown quantities. Being unknown, they create dark clouds of fear in our minds and hearts. That is why it is so hard, even for God himself, to bring off substantive change in Christ's church, to say nothing of revolution. We simply do not know, personally or institutionally, where such change, such revolution, might lead us. The unknown frightens us. The unknown has always frightened man. The unknown will always frighten man.

The unknown, however, has also a long and honorable history of fascination for man. Again and again, that fascination has led man into greatness. For there is always something stronger in man than his fear. That greater something which finally redeems, enobles, and utilizes his fear, making it an instrument of maturity, is man's faith—the kind and quality of faith that enable man to make his fear of the unknown integral to his own growth.

The evidence is piling up that we in the church are standing on the borders of a new age, an age of faith. The age we now enter is not the age of anxiety, nor the age of despair, of chaos, of detachment. It is a new age of faith that faces and feels all the fear of the unknown but does not turn back. Specifically and magnificently that new age we now enter is one of faith in Jesus Christ sovereignly and secularly revealed. We shall find, know, serve, and believe him on stormy seas of the unknown where everything we hold dear is in felt danger of destruction by raging gales of change, disturbance, and revolution.

It is the glory of man that he can enter and is entering such

151

an age. It is the glory of man that he is beginning to live in a creative state of vulnerability to the openness and the aliveness of Life. He will not die, not even when the experiences of death he fashions for himself offer the certainty, the security, and the safety of the known, the familiar, the predictable. It is the glory of man that he is robbing his institutions, specifically the church, of their power to dehumanize him, and that in so doing he is restoring those institutions to the faithful service of their original and noblest purposes. By faith in the sovereign, secular Christ, he is ushering in the new age, validating the new creation, the new being, the new Kingdom which that Christ is building in the secular world, and in our own vibrantly secular hearts. It is the glory of man even as it is the hallmark of the new age that man is incorporating the secular Christ's resurrection power into his own experience, making life whole at its roots. In the dawning age of faith man is rising from the dead to live in the real world, the only world there is, and he is there not as a robot, an automaton, nor as a slave, but as a free, responsible, creative agent and representative of his sovereign, secular Lord, ready for adventure.

To be alive in the church today reminds me of a passage in Bernaard DeVoto's *Year of Decision: 1846.* In that year not many men could give many details about the geography of those areas which now include the states of New Mexico, Arizona, Utah, Nevada, California, Wyoming, Colorado, Oregon, Washington, and Idaho.

It is of absolute importance that no map maker . . . , even if he had been able to bound these vast areas correctly, could have filled them in. Certain trails, certain rivers, long stretches of certain mountain ranges, the compass bearings of certain peaks and watersheds, the areas inhabited by certain Indian tribes—these could have been correctly indicated by the most knowledgeful, say Thomas Hart Benton and the aged Albert Gallatin. But there were exceedingly few of these and the pure white paper which the best of them would have had to leave between the known marks

152

of orientation would have extended, in the maps drawn by anyone else, from the Missouri River and central Texas, with only the slightest breaks, all the way to the Pacific. That blank paper would almost certainly have been lettered: "Great American Desert." [1]

Such is the feel of adventure, of fear, of hope, of mystery, and of faith which God-in-Christ has brought to the church in our time. As we in the church stand on the borders of that "great American desert"—the world—we know what it is to be afraid. But we also know what it is to hope, to trust, and to anticipate with joy the exploration of places we have never even dreamed about.

We have a notion or two about what lies immediately ahead. But there our knowledge ends. All the rest is un-traveled, unknown, unmapped territory. Equipped only with our love for Christ, our love for one another, and our love for the world, we stand together on the edge of discovery.

[1] Bernard DeVoto, *Year of Decision: 1846* (Boston: Little, Brown and Company, 1943), p. 6.

Epilogue

But if Christ is the One who makes
all things new, we must be prepared to
seek, find, love, serve, and worship him
where he is—
in the newness which is his creation.

Manifestly we are not prepared for this.
For the New threatens.
The New unmasks.
The New reveals the passion of our
love affair with that which is
no longer possible. Embraced,
that impossibility digs graves
where the Old conceives fear. And yet——

Fear or no fear,
he remains the One who makes all things new.
Only in newness is he changeless.
Only there. Only there. Only in what is
ever emerging, ill defined, unknown
can we rest. Only there.

So we climb out, inch by painful inch,
rebels against death,
saying "yes" to the unknown,
embracing what frightens us, opting for Life,
believing
that he understands himself—even if
we can't, or won't—when he
checks in as
the One who makes all things new.

Emerging from those graves of our
own making, we fill them with the
lovely, beautiful dirt of
resurrection power, make them
level with Life. That earth is
the Lord's and the fullness thereof.
Alleluia!
Let us hope for companions
and
be ready for anything—the best and the worst.
After all,
grave-filling is a risky business.

DATE DUE

JA 27 '70